First World War
and Army of Occupation
War Diary
France, Belgium and Germany

33 DIVISION
Headquarters, Branches and Services
Royal Army Veterinary Corps
Assistant Director Veterinary Services
12 November 1915 - 31 March 1919

WO95/2412/2

The Naval & Military Press Ltd
www.nmarchive.com
Published in association with The National Archives

Published by

The Naval & Military Press Ltd

Unit 10 Ridgewood Industrial Park,
Uckfield, East Sussex,
TN22 5QE England
Tel: +44 (0) 1825 749494

www.naval-military-press.com
www.nmarchive.com

This diary has been reprinted in facsimile from the original. Any imperfections are inevitably reproduced and the quality may fall short of modern type and cartographic standards.

© Crown Copyright
Images reproduced by permission of The National Archives, London, England, 2015.

Contents

Document type	Place/Title	Date From	Date To
Heading	WO95/2412/2		
Heading	33rd Division Divl Troops Asst Dir. Vety Services. Nov 1915 Mar 1919		
Heading	H.Q. 33rd Div. A.D.R.S. Vol I Nov 15-Feb 19		
War Diary		12/11/1915	30/11/1915
Heading	A.D.V.S. 33rd Div. Vol 2		
War Diary	Busnes	01/12/1915	02/12/1915
War Diary	Bethune	03/12/1915	06/12/1915
War Diary	Busnes	01/12/1915	02/12/1915
War Diary	Bethune	03/12/1915	12/12/1915
War Diary	Busnes	13/12/1915	31/12/1915
Heading	A.D.V.S 33rd Div. Vol. 3 Jan 16		
War Diary	Bethune	01/01/1916	31/01/1916
Heading	A.D.V.S. 33rd Div. Vol. 4		
War Diary	Bethune	01/02/1916	29/02/1916
Heading	A.D.V.S 33rd Div. Vol 5		
War Diary	Bethune	09/03/1916	06/07/1916
War Diary	Treux	15/07/1916	15/07/1916
War Diary	Meaulte	16/07/1916	18/07/1916
War Diary	Bethune	07/07/1916	08/07/1916
War Diary	Belloy	10/07/1916	11/07/1916
War Diary	Corbie	12/07/1916	12/07/1916
War Diary	Treux	13/07/1916	14/07/1916
War Diary	Meaulte	18/07/1916	21/07/1916
War Diary	Camp Near Meaulte	22/07/1916	22/07/1916
War Diary	Ribemont	23/07/1916	23/07/1916
War Diary	Treux	24/07/1916	25/07/1916
War Diary	Camp	26/07/1916	31/07/1916
War Diary	Buire	01/08/1916	06/08/1916
War Diary	Albert Road	07/08/1916	31/08/1916
War Diary	Nillers-Bocage	01/09/1916	01/09/1916
War Diary	Bernaville	02/09/1916	03/09/1916
War Diary	Frohen-Le-Grand	04/09/1916	04/09/1916
War Diary	Flers	05/09/1916	08/09/1916
War Diary	Pas	09/09/1916	21/09/1916
War Diary	Henu	22/09/1916	29/09/1916
War Diary	Doullens	30/09/1916	10/10/1916
War Diary	Corbie	19/10/1916	21/10/1916
War Diary	Treux	22/10/1916	22/10/1916
War Diary	F21.B Central	23/10/1916	25/10/1916
War Diary	A.2.D.9.7	26/10/1916	08/11/1916
War Diary	Treux	09/11/1916	10/11/1916
War Diary	Hallencourt	11/11/1916	05/12/1916
War Diary	Albert	06/12/1916	15/12/1916
War Diary	L.16.D.1.9	16/12/1916	28/12/1916
War Diary	Long	29/12/1916	31/12/1916
Heading	R.A. Plunkett Major AVC A.D.V.S 33 Division		
War Diary	Long	01/01/1917	18/01/1917
War Diary	Chipilly	19/01/1917	25/01/1917
War Diary	Suzanne	26/01/1917	08/03/1917

War Diary	Corbie	09/03/1917	31/03/1917
War Diary	In The Field	01/04/1917	31/01/1919
Heading	War Diary Of D.A.D.V.S. 33rd Division For February 1919 Original Vol 41		
War Diary	In The Field	01/02/1919	28/02/1919
War Diary	Etretat	01/03/1919	04/03/1919
War Diary	Andainville	05/03/1919	06/03/1919
War Diary	Etretat	07/03/1919	31/03/1919

WO 95/24122

33RD DIVISION
DIVL TROOPS

ASST DIR. VETY SERVICES.
NOV 1915 - ~~FEB~~ 1919
MAR

33RD DIVISION
DIVL TROOPS

Ap. 33 దస్త్రి,
A.సి.ర.స.
Vol I

131/7694

ans

Nov. 15
Dec. 19

WAR DIARY or INTELLIGENCE SUMMARY

(Erase heading not required.)

Army Form C. 2118

from A.D.V.S., 33rd Division.

Place	Date 1915	Hour	Summary of Events and Information	Remarks and references to Appendices
	12/11	noon	Entrained at AMESBURY.	
	"	2.0 pm	Detrained at SOUTHAMPTON. Embarked on S.S. "MAIDAN."	
	"	4.0 pm		
	15/11	4.0 pm	Disembarked at LE HAVRE.	A.V.P.
	16/11	2.0 am	Entrained at LE HAVRE.	A.V.P.
	17/11	1.0 am	Detrained at STEENBECQUE, marched to MORBECQUES. Office opened at MORBECQUES. (Balance of Div. Headquarters Staff arrived.)	A.V.P.
	18/11		Order to move to BUSNES cancelled at last minute. Office reopened. 100th Brigade (Infantry) arrived.	A.V.P.
	19/11		98th Infantry Brigade move to BETHUNE from BUSNES area. 100th Field Ambulance arrived. 4.3rd Mobile Veterinary Section report arrival.	A.V.P.
	20/11		98th Infantry Brigade attached to 2nd and 4th Divisions for training. 101st Field Ambulance arrived. 18th Middlesex (Pioneer) Battalion attached 4th Division for training.	A.V.P.
	21/11		Ordinary Office duties.	A.V.P.
	22/11			A.V.P.
	23/11		Marched with Divl. Headquarters Staff from MORBECQUES to BUSNES. Office opened in Rue du Chateau, BUSNES.	A.V.P.
	24/11		Outbreak of Mange in B. Squadron, North Irish Horse affecting animals and 2 in-contacts evacuated by 4.3rd Mobile Veterinary Section.	A.V.P.

WAR DIARY
or
INTELLIGENCE SUMMARY

Army Form C. 2118

(Erase heading not required.)

Instructions regarding War Diaries and Intelligence Summaries are contained in F.S. Regs., Part II. and the Staff Manual respectively. Title Pages will be prepared in manuscript.

Place	Date 1915	Hour	Summary of Events and Information	Remarks and references to Appendices
	24/11		Continued:- All the necessary instructions to prevent spread of disease issued to O/C Squadrons.	W.D.
	25/11		In company with O/C 4 & 5 Mobile Sections, inspected horses left behind in billets by units at BOESEGHEM, BLARINGHEM, STEENBECQUES, MORBECQUES and HAZEBROUCK. 99th Infantry Brigade and 100th Field Ambulance transferred to 2nd Division. 19th Infantry Brigade and 19th Field Ambulance transferred to 33rd Division.	W.D.
	26/11		Inspected Horse and sick lines of 4 & 3pe Mobile Veterinary Sections, instructed V.O's. as to more immediate and routine of cases left behind for attention by Mobile Section.	W.D.
	27/11		Visited E.V.C. a charger which was left behind at MORBECQUES suffering from pneumonia. Instructed V.O.S. to look into information and details as to how they are standing, also when transferred to charge of myself or other V. Officer, assume me the name of officer, and several transfers of animals i.e. speering, firestorm from contagion to and whether the Brits may kept up. If present.	W.D.
	28/11		Inspected Horse of 18th Mindley (Pioneer) Battalion, — assumed instructions re treatment of animals O.C. to Transport Officer.	W.D.
	29/11		Instructing piermen from A.A.V.S. 1st Army (289. V.S.) are attached too long before being concepted, who is therefore exhausted nothing and being incur by desirable by Veterinary Officer.	W.D.

WAR DIARY
or
INTELLIGENCE SUMMARY

(Erase heading not required.)

Army Form C. 2118

Place	Date 1915	Hour	Summary of Events and Information	Remarks and references to Appendices
	30/11		Inspected Horse Lines of 99th and 101st Field Ambulances, Divisional Ammunition Column Signatory Ry. Horses in No 2. Section include animals which were in unsatisfactory condition; reported & matter to CRA asking him to enquire into cause of unfitness.	

W. R. Crundett
Major RC
A.D.V.S. 33rd Division.

30-11-15

Astr. 33rd Stri.
vol: 2

7978/71

and

Duplicate

WAR DIARY
INTELLIGENCE SUMMARY
(Erase heading not required.)

Army Form C. 2118

for December 1915
of — A.D.V.S., 33rd Division

Place	Date 1915	Hour	Summary of Events and Information	Remarks and references to Appendices
BUSNES	1/12	—	Outbreak of Mange in 101st Field Ambulance. Animal evacuated. All units inspected, and necessary reports made, and instructions issued.	1/1 A.D?
	2/12	—	Moved from BUSNES to BETHUNE and established office at 2 Rue l'Ermitage. Evacuated horse suffering from suspicious skin disease — probably Mange — from Headquarters Company, 33rd Divisional Train; issued necessary instructions to avoid spread of disease, and wire reports to those concerned.	1/1 A.D?
BETHUNE	3/12		Inspected animals of "L" Squadron North Irish Horse; general conditions good, and shewing up to date.	1/1 A.D?
"	4/12		Inspected lines of 33rd Signal Company; found them in a very dirty condition. Lack of Lime — materially checks cleaning of lines reported to A.D.M.G. for information of G.O.C. Inspected lines of 99th Field Ambulance; also 19th and 101st. Shewing of 99th bad. O/C same as reason "make & get able". Instructed him to meet Inspect Officer A.D.M.S. and sent to have some horses. Report of inspection sent A.D.M.S.	1/1 A.D?
"	5/12		Inspected horses of Divisional Headquarters staff, including M.M.P. All animals looking well, and shewing up to date	1/1 A.D?
"	6/12		Visited Headquarters Company, 33rd Divisional Train. Found a number of sick horses & suffering from sore necks. Necessary instructions issued to those concerned illustrating treatment and sanitation.	1/1 A.D?

Army Form C. 2118

WAR DIARY for December, 1915

INTELLIGENCE SUMMARY of
— A.D.V.S., 33rd Division

(Erase heading not required.)

Instructions regarding War Diaries and Intelligence Summaries are contained in F.S. Regs., Part II. and the Staff Manual respectively. Title Pages will be prepared in manuscript.

Place	Date 1915	Hour	Summary of Events and Information	Remarks and references to Appendices
BUSNES	1/12	—	Outbreak of Mange in 101st Field Ambulance. Animal evacuated. All went inspected, and necessary reports made, and instructions issued.	1/MP
—	2/12	—	Moved from BUSNES to BETHUNE and established office at 2 Rue l'Ermitage. Evacuated horse suffering from a suspicious skin disease – probably Mange – from Headquarters Company, 33rd Divisional Train; issued necessary instructions to avoid spread of disease, and made reports to those concerned.	1/MP
BETHUNE	3/12	—	Inspected animals of "L" Squadron North Irish Horse; general condition good, and shoeing up-to-date.	1/MP
"	4/12	—	Inspected lines of 33rd Signal Company, R.E. Found them in a very dirty condition. Lack of time – information of EIC. reported Brig. Genl. Inspected horses of 99th Field Ambulance also 19th and 101st. Shoeing of 99th bad. O/C gave as reason "unable to get shoes". Instructed him to indent twice in usual amount. Three shoeings done weekly. Report of inspection sent to A.D.M.S.	1/MP
—	5/12	—	Inspected horses of Divisional Headquarters Staff, including M.M.P. All animals looking well, and shoeing up-to-date.	1/MP
—	6/12	—	Visited Headquarters Company, 33rd Divisional Train. Found a number of sick horses suffering from sore necks and mountainous sores. Three concerned attending treatment and isolation	1/MP

Army Form C. 2118

WAR DIARY
INTELLIGENCE SUMMARY
(Erase heading not required.)

Instructions regarding War Diaries and Intelligence Summaries are contained in F.S. Regs., Part II. and the Staff Manual respectively. Title Pages will be prepared in manuscript.

Place	Date	Hour	Summary of Events and Information	Remarks and references to Appendices
BETHUNE	7/12		Inspected horses and lines of 42nd & 43rd Mule Veterinary Sections, and lines of Divisional Remount's Staff horses.	1/12?
"	8/12		One suspected mange and one "in contact" encountered from 62nd Brigade R.A. Inspected remainder of animals in unit found them clean looking well, shewing up to date.	11/12?
			One horse suffering from a suspicious skin disease – probably Mange – encountered from 1/2 East Anglian Brigade R.F.A. No contact could be traced. Must inspect.	?
"	9/12		Instructions received from D.D.V.S. that all animals are to be examined by the Intra-Arrival Palpebral method (396 V.S.) Reactions or suspicious reactions to be reported by wire. Examined M.O's charger at C.R.E's Stables, insanitary condition. Stated reported to C.R.E's Adjutant. Examined animal suffering from a suspicious skin disease at No.3 Company train, encountered 2 animals to Mobile Section, and search all mastication to these concerned as everything to Reports out all concerned. Journey brought up this animal from this suffering from sore cracked animals the worked exposed, kept on inhalation, clipped all and scrubbed.	11/12?

1875. Wt. W5931/1116. 1,020,000. 4/15. J.B.C. & A. A.D.S.S./Forms/C. 2118.

Army Form C. 2118

WAR DIARY
INTELLIGENCE SUMMARY
(Erase heading not required.)

Instructions regarding War Diaries and Intelligence Summaries are contained in F. S. Regs., Part II. and the Staff Manual respectively. Title Pages will be prepared in manuscript.

Place	Date 1915	Hour	Summary of Events and Information	Remarks and references to Appendices
BETHUNE	10/12		Inspected 30 horses on transfer from Ammunition Column, 64th Brigade R.F.A. to 33rd Divisional Train. Inspected horses prepared for evacuation to Base from 43rd Mobile Veterinary Section.	MAP?
"	11/12		Ordinary Office duties.	MAP?
"	12/12		Moved from BETHUNE to BUSNES. Office now established at BUSNES by 12.0 noon. Examined pneumonia case left behind by 1st Cameronians with 6th West Kents. Arrived A.D.V.S., 12th Division of Cav. 101st Field Ambulance and met Section, 4th Reserve Park remaining at BETHUNE: A.D.V.S. 12th Division arranged. One animal evacuation from "F"Squadron North Irish Horse suffering from a crupting skin eruption; the animal was on indirect contact with other cases of this Squadron and has been isolated since November 24th. All veterinary cases and reports sent.	MAP?
BUSNES	13/12		Inspected billets occupied by horses of "F" Squadron North Irish Horse, and 212th Field Company, R.E. Generally conditions good.	MAP?
"	14/12		Inspected billets of horses of 1st Cameronians and found them in a dirty condition. Arrived of 33rd Divisional Artillery reported. Asked C.R.A. to instruct V.O.s to report to me.	MAP?
"	15/12		Saw all horses of 18th Middlesex (Pioneer) Battalion. General condition of animals good, and shewing up well. Billets of horses were clean.	MAP

1875 Wt. W593/826 1,000,000 4/15 J.B.C. & A. A.D.S.S./Forms/C. 2118.

Army Form C. 2118

WAR DIARY
INTELLIGENCE SUMMARY
(Erase heading not required.)

Place	Date 1915.	Hour	Summary of Events and Information	Remarks and references to Appendices
BUSNES	16/12		Parade of animals of 96th Infantry Brigade Headqrs, 99th Field Ambulance and No 3 Coy; 33rd Divisional Train. General condition of animals of the 2 first mentioned units very good, those of No 3 Coy: fair. All animals were well shod.	M.M.P.
"	17/12		Conference of V.O's. Practical demonstration of intra-renal palpebral method of malleinization. Mallein and syringes received; malleinization commenced.	M.M.P.
"	18/12		Inspecting horses under mallein test; no reactions	M.M.P.
"	19/12		Parade of animals of 222 Company, R.E. Shoeing bad. Report sent C.R.E.	M.M.P.
"	20/12		Inspecting animals under mallein test; no reactions.	M.M.P.
"	21/12		Parade of animals of 18th Royal Fusiliers, 19th Field Ambulance, 16th Middlesex, and 11th Field Company, R.E. Shoeing of animals in 18th R.F. very bad: reported Brigade Headquarters. 2nd application to Remts School for animals for training orderlies.	M.P.
"	22/12		Inspected animals of 16th Kings Royal Rifles and 20th Royal Fusiliers. General condition and shoeing good.	M.P.

WAR DIARY
INTELLIGENCE SUMMARY
(Erase heading not required.)

Army Form C. 2118

Place	Date 1915.	Hour	Summary of Events and Information	Remarks and references to Appendices
BUSNES	23/12		Inspected horse lines of 33rd Divisional Ammunition Column. General condition fair, showing good. Horse lines dirty.	11 a.D.
"	24/12.		Parade of animals of 19th Royal Irish(?). Animals looking well and shod up-to-date. Exceptionally clean condition of horse lines reported. Brigade Headquarters. Inspected horse lines of 21st Royal Irish(?). Battalion re their dirty condition. Report sent O/C	11 a.D.
"	25/12.		Inspecting horses under mallein test.	11 a.D.
"	26/12		"	11 a.D.
"	27/12.		On report from Veterinary Officer in charge, examined a number of horses in 156 Brigade R.F.A. and found them to be suffering from lice. Inspected personnel (including kit and equipment) of 4/3rd Mobile Veterinary Section. Arrangements made for men to have a bath.	11 a.D.
"	28/12.		Examined sporadic cases of suspicious skin disease awaiting examination by Mobile Section.	11 a.D.

Army Form C. 2118

WAR DIARY
INTELLIGENCE SUMMARY
(Erase heading not required.)

Instructions regarding War Diaries and Intelligence Summaries are contained in F. S. Regs., Part II. and the Staff Manual respectively. Title Pages will be prepared in manuscript.

Place	Date 19/5	Hour	Summary of Events and Information	Remarks and references to Appendices
BUSNES	29/12		Parade of animals of Batteries, 162nd Brigade R.F.A. Horses looking well. Shoeing fair.	Nil
	30/12		Moved with Divisional Headquarters from BUSNES to BETHUNE. Office established in room vacated by A.D.V.S., 2nd Division.	Nil
	31/12		Ordinary Routine duties.	Nil

W. Rothwell Major A.V.C.
A.D.V.S., 33rd Division.

Asib. 33 stir.
Vol 3
The Tile

Army Form C. 2118

WAR DIARY
or
INTELLIGENCE SUMMARY
(Erase heading not required.) OF MAJOR R.A. PLUNKETT, AVC, ADVS, 33rd DIVISION.

for JANUARY, 1916

Place	Date 1916 JAN.	Hour	Summary of Events and Information	Remarks and references to Appendices
BETHUNE	1st	—	Inspected animals of 33rd Divisional Ammunition Column. All the animals in fair condition, and well shod.	N.A.P.
"	2	—	Parade of horses of 19th and 99th Field Ambulances and 33rd Divisional Cyclists. All animals looking well.	N.A.P.
"	3	—	Parade of animals of 1 Squadron, North Irish Horse. Shoeing and condition good, discussed several lame horses in the ranks. Inspected animals of 212th Field Coy. R.E. condition good, shoeing bad: — reported D.H.Q.	N.A.P.
"	4		Routine and Office duties.	N.A.P.
"	5		Inspected horse lines and animals of 21st Royal Fusiliers and No 3 Section. Condition and shoeing fair.	N.A.P.
"	6		Visited C Battery, 167 Brigade R.F.A. at LE QUESNOY. Examined cases of suspicious skin disease with remainder of this Brigade, and found them to be suffering from Lice. Report, and instructions re treatment sent C.R.A.	N.A.P.
"	7		Ordinary Routine and Office duties.	N.A.P.
"	8		Visited 162 and 166 Brigades R.F.A. and Headquarters Company, 33rd Divl. Train.	N.A.P. N.A.P.

WAR DIARY or INTELLIGENCE SUMMARY

Army Form C. 2118

Place	Date 1916 JAN.	Hour	Summary of Events and Information	Remarks and references to Appendices
BETHUNE	9	-	Ordinary Routine and Office duties.	W.W.R
"	10	-	Inspected animals of 20th Royal Fusiliers and 33rd Signal Coy: R.E. General condition good, animals dirty.	W.W.R
"	11	-	Ordinary Routine duties	W.W.R
"	12	-	Inspected horse lines of 1st Conveyors, and care of animals of No 3 Section, 4th Reserve Park.	W.W.R
"	13	-	Ordinary Routine and Office duties.	W.W.R
"	14	-	"	W.W.R
"	15	-	Inspected animals of 98th Infantry Brigade. General condition and shoeing good. Visited Headquarters, 156 Brigade R.F.A. and B Battery, 166 Brigade R.F.A.	W.W.R

Army Form C. 2118

WAR DIARY
INTELLIGENCE SUMMARY
(Erase heading not required.)

Instructions regarding War Diaries and Intelligence Summaries are contained in F.S. Regs., Part II. and the Staff Manual respectively. Title Pages will be prepared in manuscript.

Place	Date 1916 JAN.	Hour	Summary of Events and Information	Remarks and references to Appendices
BETHUNE	16	—	Ordinary Routine and Office duties.	W.M?
"	17	—	Inspected No 3 Company, 33rd Divl. Train, also animals of 16th Middlesex. The latter were feeding the animals off the ground — reported the matter to the G.O.C. Brigade. Visited Remount Depot, GONNEHEM, regarding cart horses.	W.M?
"	18.		Visited Headquarters Company, 33rd Divisional Train and inspected animals of 33rd Divisional Ammunition Column. All animals looking well.	W.M?
"	19		Ordinary Routine and Office duties.	W.M?
"	20		Visited C.R.A. at BUSNES	W.M?
"	21		Inspected horses of 1st Queens, and 25 animals of 1st Middlesex Transport. Committee sat.	W.M?

Army Form C. 2118

WAR DIARY
or
INTELLIGENCE SUMMARY
(Erase heading not required.)

Instructions regarding War Diaries and Intelligence Summaries are contained in F.S. Regs., Part II. and the Staff Manual respectively. Title Pages will be prepared in manuscript.

Place	Date 1916. JANY.	Hour	Summary of Events and Information	Remarks and references to Appendices
BETHUNE	22	—	Inspected animals of 16th Kings Royal Rifles. Horses looking well, shoeing fair.	A.V.C.
"	23		Ordinary Routine and Office duties.	A.V.C.
"	24		"	A.V.C.
"	25		Visited Lt. Egan AVC at his billet; temporarily indisposed. Instructed Capt. Leese AVC to take temporary charge of his animals.	A.V.C.
"	26.		Visited C.R.A. re general condition of animals in R.F.A. Brigades under his command, and also regarding sick returns for horses. Conference of all V.O's of R.F.A. Brigades regarding their duties.	A.V.C.
"			Inspected shoes returned to Divisional armoury unit by R.F.A. Brigades; in compliance with Divisional Routine Orders.	A.V.C.

WAR DIARY
or
INTELLIGENCE SUMMARY
(Erase heading not required.)

Army Form C. 2118

Place	Date 1916. JAN.	Hour	Summary of Events and Information	Remarks and references to Appendices
BETHUNE	27	—	Ordinary Routine & Office duties.	W.A.R.
"	28	—	Parade of all animals in Nos 2, 3 & 4 Coys 33rd Divisional Train. All horses looking well, and shod up to date.	W.A.R.
"	29	—	Ordinary Routine duties.	W.A.R.
"	30	—	Inspected lines & animals of 33rd Signal Co. R.E. Animals in fair condition & well shod, but dirty.	W.A.R.
"	31	—	Inspected animals of 156 and 166 Brigades R.F.A. on the line of march. Stabling of animals in 156 Brigade very bad.	W.A.R.

Add. 33ʳᵈ &c.
vol. 4

Army Form C. 2118

WAR DIARY
or
INTELLIGENCE SUMMARY

(Erase heading not required.)

WAR DIARY for February, 1916
OF Major Chudkutt A.V.C. 33 Division

Place	Date 1916 FEB	Hour	Summary of Events and Information	Remarks and references to Appendices
BETHUNE	1st		At the request of the adjutant 69nd Bde R.F.A., I inspected some animals in the Ammunition Column of this brigade. There were several suffering from lice.	U.B.A.
"	2nd		Inspected the lines of the 1st Cameronians and 18th Fusiliers, where I found all the animals looking well and the shoeing satisfactory.	U.B.A.
"	3		Routine and office duties	U.B.A.
"	4		Parade of animals 2nd Royal Welsh Fusiliers the number of animals I noticed were losing condition. The necessary instructions regarding these animals were given those concerned.	U.B.A.
"	5		Visited the 101st Field Ambulance and found the condition and shoeing of the animals good.	U.B.A.
"	6		Inspected the lines of 19th & 99th Field Ambulance. The shoeing of the 99th is satisfactory but that of the 19th needs improvement. The condition of all animals was fair.	U.B.A.

Army Form C. 2118

WAR DIARY for February 1916
INTELLIGENCE SUMMARY

(Erase heading not required.) of Major R.A. Plunkett A.V.C. 33rd Division.

Place	Date 1916 Feb.	Hour	Summary of Events and Information	Remarks and references to Appendices
Bethune	7		Inspected a few sick animals at 33rd Divisional Headquarter Company Train	W.A.P.
"	8		In conjunction with V.O. R.F.A. Brigade 33rd Division, retested by the Intra-dermal Ophthalmic method, the animals of the 166th Brigade R.F.A. Inspected animals of 156 Bygrave R.F.A. Condition extra satisfactory.	W.A.P.
"	9		Ordinary Routine and Office duties.	W.A.P.
"	10		Inspected the animals of 166th Bde. R.F.A. under tent.	W.A.P.
"	11		Parade of animals of the 167 Bde R.F.A. shoeing fair.	W.A.P.
"	12		Inspected in company with D.D.V.S. 1st Army doubtfull reactor to mallein 166 Bde R.F.A. Animal destroyed.	W.A.P.
"	13		Visited the lines of 32nd Brigade R.G.A. General condition and shoeing good.	W.A.P.
"	14		Inspected all animals of 163 Bde R.F.A. and 33rd D.A.C. The condition of animals very good, also shoeing.	W.A.P.

Army Form C. 2118

WAR DIARY for February 1916
or
INTELLIGENCE SUMMARY
(Erase heading not required.) of Major R.A. Plunkett A.V.C. 33rd Division

Instructions regarding War Diaries and Intelligence Summaries are contained in F.S. Regs., Part II. and the Staff Manual respectively. Title Pages will be prepared in manuscript.

Place	Date 1916 Feb.	Hour	Summary of Events and Information	Remarks and references to Appendices
Bethune	15		Ordinary routine office duties	R.A.P.
"	16		Visited the lines of 23rd Brigade R.G.A. Shoeing bad in one battery.	R.A.P.
"	17		Inspected the lines 7th Bde R.G.A. condition and shoeing satisfactory	R.A.P.
"	18		Had the animals of the 21st R.Fusiliers trotted by, and inspected the horse lines of this unit. Lines in very bad state, condition of animals fair. Shoeing good.	R.A.P.
"	19		Ordinary routine and office duties	R.A.P.
"	20		Attended parade of all animals in 7th & sections 1st Bridging train and the Hants Fortress Coy. General appearance moderate, all animals shod up to date.	R.A.P.
"	21		Inspected Advanced 1st Army Signals, horses and lines, all animals looking well, shoeing fair.	R.A.P.

WAR DIARY for February 1916
or
INTELLIGENCE SUMMARY
(Erase heading not required.) of Major R.A. Plunkett A.V.C. 33rd Division

Army Form C. 2118

Instructions regarding War Diaries and Intelligence Summaries are contained in F.S. Regs., Part II. and the Staff Manual respectively. Title Pages will be prepared in manuscript.

Place	Date 1916 Feb	Hour	Summary of Events and Information	Remarks and references to Appendices
Bethune	22		Ordinary routine and office duties. Visited the 1/6 Scots Rifles, who have just been attached to the division	W.R.P. W.R.P.
"	23		Ordinary routine and office duties.	W.R.P.
"	24			
"	25		Main body of 33rd divisional artillery move to gun line. Interviewed Major Andrews A.V.C. A.D.V.S. 16th division.	W.R.P.
"	26		Ordinary routine and office duties.	W.R.P.
"	27		Conference with V.O's. Parade of animals 7th & 8th sections 1st Bridging Train	W.R.P.
"	28		Went on leave. Capt Lalor A.V.C. assisted by A.D.V.S 2nd Division is acting during my absence.	W.R.P.
"	29		On leave.	W.R.P.

W.R. Plunkett
Major A.V.C.

ADVS
33/2DW
Vol 5

Army Form C. 2118

WAR DIARY for March, 1916
or
INTELLIGENCE SUMMARY

(Erase heading not required.)

of Major Plunkett, APC, attchd 33rd Div.

Place	Date 1916.	Hour	Summary of Events and Information	Remarks and references to Appendices
BETHUNE	9.3.16		March 1st to 8th inclusive. — On leave.	J.H.P.
"	10.3.16		Ordinary Routine Office duties.	J.H.P.
"	11.3.16		Visited Lines inspected animals of 156 Brigade R.F.A. Majority of animals clean & in good condition.	J.H.P.
"	12.3.16		Ordinary Routine Office duties.	J.H.P.
"	13.3.16		Inspected animals of Divisional Headquarters Staff, which were all entering well.	J.H.P.
"	14.3.16		Inspected animals of 166 Brigade R.F.A. and 1 Section of the 33rd Divisional Ammunition Column.	J.H.P.
"	15.3.16		Visited Horse Lines and examined the animals of the 4th King's Liverpool Regiment. Animals in good condition throng up to date. Walked round the Lines and inspected all the animals of the 162 Brigade R.F.A. and the 4th Suffolks. General condition showing good.	J.H.P.

WAR DIARY for March, 1916 Army Form C. 2118
INTELLIGENCE SUMMARY — continued
(Erase heading not required.)

Place	Date 1916	Hour	Summary of Events and Information	Remarks and references to Appendices
	16.3.16	—	Ordinary Routine office duties.	
	17.3.16	—	Visited Horse Lines. Inspected animals of 167 Brigade R.F.A. and the auxiliary Horse Transport. The lines of a Battery 167 Brigade R.F.A. were in a dirty condition. A few thin horses were noticed by me in this Brigade; otherwise general condition showing good.	
	18.3.16		Conference of Veterinary Officers of the Division and Corps Troops attached, at my office.	
	19.3.16		Inspected site for Mobile Section billet in Reserve Area. The same of the Division to Reserve Area was afterwards postponed indefinitely.	
	20.3.16		Mounted Parade, fully equipped, of all A.V.C. Sergeants attached to units of the Division. These N.C.O.'s presented a smart appearance on parade, and the majority are well mounted.	
	21.3.16		Inspected Infirmary animals of the 33rd Divisional Ammunition Column.	

WAR DIARY for March, 1916.

INTELLIGENCE SUMMARY — continued

(Erase heading not required.)

Army Form C. 2118

Place	Date 1916.	Hour	Summary of Events and Information	Remarks and references to Appendices
	22.3.16		Parade of animals of the 33rd Divisional Train, a/c. General condition of all animals good. Shoeing up to date.	11/10
	23.3.16		Ordinary Routine office duties.	11/10
	24.3.16		Inspected Lines & animals of O.O. Cable Section. R.E. 11th Corps. Shoeing bad, condition of horses moderate.	11/10
	25.3.16		18th Parade of animals of No. 9 Machine Gun Squadron. Condition of animals fair, shoeing very bad. Conference of all V.O's at my office.	11/10
	26.3.16		Visit of D.D.V.S., 1st Army.	11/10
	27.3.16		Inspected animals of O.O. Cable Section R.E. XI Corps.	11/10
	28.3.16		Walked round Lines & inspected animals of 1/6 Scots Rifles and 33rd Signal Company R.E.	11/10

WAR DIARY for March, 1916. — continued —
INTELLIGENCE SUMMARY — continued —
(Erase heading not required.)

Army Form C. 2118

Place	Date 1916	Hour	Summary of Events and Information	Remarks and references to Appendices
	29.3.16		Parade of animals of 11th, 212th, 222nd and 227th field Companies R.E. General conditions and shoeing good.	M.C.
	30.3.16		Walked round the Lines inspected animals of 1st Canadians and the 19th Brigade Machine Gun Section.	M.C.
	31.3.16		Ordinary Routine office duties.	M.C.
	3.4.16.			

W.R. Burnett
Major A.V.C.
A.D.V.S., 33rd Division.

Army Form C. 2118

WAR DIARY
INTELLIGENCE SUMMARY
(Erase heading not required.)

for April 1916 of
Major R.E. Plunkett, A.V.C.,
A.D.V.S., 33rd Division Vol 6

Place	Date 1916	Hour	Summary of Events and Information	Remarks and references to Appendices
BETHUNE	1-4.		Inspected lines animals of 1st QUEENS. Conference with Veterinary Officer.	M.D.
— do —	2-4.		Inspected lines animals of Ammunition Column, 162 Brigade R.F.A. and 19, 99th and 101st Field Ambulances. Both the lines animals of the Column/162 Brigade appeared to be in front condition.	M.D.
— do —	3-4.		Walked round the horse lines of A Battery, 164 and B Battery, 156 Brigade R.F.A.	M.D.
— do —	4-4.		Inspected animals of B Battery, 156 Brigade R.F.A. A number of the animals appeared to be losing condition and special instructions were issued regarding the treatment of these animals.	M.D.
— do —	5-4.		Walked round lines of Column, 162 Brigade R.F.A.	M.D.
— do —	6-4.		Examined the animals Inspected horse lines of 16th Notts & Derbys + 19 K.R.R. who were attached to Division for training.	M.D.

WAR DIARY for APRIL, 1916.

Army Form C. 2118

Major R.A. Plunkett, A.V.C.

INTELLIGENCE SUMMARY

A.D.V.S. 33rd DIVN.

Place	Date 1916	Hour	Summary of Events and Information	Remarks and references to Appendices
BETHUNE	7.4		Ordinary routine and Office duties.	M.P.
— do —	8.4		Usual weekly conference of Veterinary Officers at the Office.	M.P.
— do —	9.4		Saw the animals of the 13th Gloucesters (Pioneer Battn.) and the 14th Notts & Derby. & 16th Rifle Brigade Trench by; later I visited the Remount Depot, GONNEHEM.	M.P.
— do —	10.4		Attended parade of all animals of 1st & 2nd Brigade R.G.A.	M.P.
— do —	11.4		Inspected lines & animals of 1st Canterinning, O.O. Calle Section R.F. II Corps; also the Ammunition Column and A, C and D Batteries, 166 Brigade R.F.A.	M.P.
— do —	12.4		Parade of animals of 20th L. Battn: Royal Fusiliers. Ordinary routine and Office duties.	M.P.
— do —	13.4		Examined animals of Ammunition Column, 169 Brigade R.F.A. On the whole the animals are looking well, but there are a number of cases cress amongst them.	M.P.

WAR DIARY or INTELLIGENCE SUMMARY
Army Form C. 2118

1st APRIL, 1916.
Major R.A. Plunkett, A.V.C.
A.D.V.S., 33rd Division.

Place	Date 1916	Hour	Summary of Events and Information	Remarks and references to Appendices
BETHUNE	14/4		Parade of animals of A. + B. Batteries, 156 Brigade R.F.A. A number of the animals are in poor condition.	11 M.O.
— do —	15/4		Inspected animals of 33rd Signal Coy; R.E. and Ammunition Column, 162 Brigade R.F.A.	11 M.O.
— do —	16/4		Attended Conference of A.D.V.S. at 1st Army Headquarters.	11 M.O.
— do —	17/4		Walked round Hy Lines of the Ammunition Column, 156 Brigade R.F.A. but the while the animals are looking well. Examined all the horses of 1 Squadron, North Irish Horse prior to their move from Divisional area to go on manœuvres.	11 M.O.
— do —	18/4		Paraded animals of A. + B. Batteries, 162 Brigade R.A. The horses are in fair condition and about up to duty.	11 M.O.

WAR DIARY for APRIL, 1916 of Major R.A. Plunkett A.V.C.
INTELLIGENCE SUMMARY
A.D.V.S., 33rd Division.

(Erase heading not required.)

Army Form C. 2118

Place	Date 1916	Hour	Summary of Events and Information	Remarks and references to Appendices
BETHUNE	19/4		Visited & inspected animals of C Battery 164 Brigade R.F.A., 18th Middlesex (Pioneers) Battn. and the 1st Cameronians; a large number of the animals in the first named unit are in poor condition, the other two units very much better, particularly the animals of the Pioneers, which looked well.	M.H.P.
-do-	19/4		Walked round the lines of the Ammunition Column 166 Brigade R.F.A. and received a visit from A.D.V.S., 1st Army who advises me of his proposal to inspect all animals in Division commencing 21st instant.	M.H.P.
-do-	20/4		Ordinary routine office duties. In conjunction with an officer from each of the units concerned, visited rendezvous for inspection of animals by D.D.V.S., and arranged the schema to be followed up by the different units.	M.H.P.
-do-	21/4		D.D.V.S., 1st Army inspects the animals of the following units: 19th and 98th Infantry Brigades	M.H.P.

Army Form C. 2118

WAR DIARY for APRIL, 1916 of Major R.A. Plunkett, A.V.C.

INTELLIGENCE SUMMARY

A.D.V.S., 33rd Division

(Erase heading not required.)

Instructions regarding War Diaries and Intelligence Summaries are contained in F. S. Regs., Part II. and the Staff Manual respectively. Title Pages will be prepared in manuscript.

Place	Date 1916	Hour	Summary of Events and Information	Remarks and references to Appendices
BETHUNE	21/4		Continued 11th, 212th and 222nd Field Companies R.E. and 18th Middlesex (Pioneers) in the morning; and the 110th Infantry Brigade, 33rd Divisional Train, 19th, 99th and 101st Field Ambulances, 33rd Signal Company R.E. and Divisional Headquarters Staff in the afternoon.	1/1 M.O.
—do—	22/4		Owing to inclement weather proposed inspection by D.D.V.S. of R.F.A. animals is postponed until 23rd instant, and inspection originally fixed up for 23rd postponed until the 25th. Ordinary Routine office duties.	1/1 M.O.
—do—	23/4		D.D.V.S., 1st Army inspects animals of following units :— 33rd D.A.C., D/162 the whole of the 166th Bde: R.F.A., Howard during lecture, also A,C, and D Batteries, 164 Brigade and B. Battery, 156 Brigade R.F.A.	11 M.O.
—do—	24/4		Ordinary Routine and office duties.	11 M.O.
—do—	25/4		D.D.V.S. inspects animals of following units :— A,C,D Batteries, 156 Brigade R.F.A., also Ammunition Column, 156 Brigade R.F.A. and	11 M.O.

WAR DIARY or INTELLIGENCE SUMMARY

Army Form C. 2118

WAR DIARY for APRIL, 1916 of Major R.A. Plunkett, A.V.C.
A.D.V.S., 33rd Division.

Place	Date 1916	Hour	Summary of Events and Information	Remarks and references to Appendices
BETHUNE	25/4		—continued— 164th Brigade R.F.A., 3rd, 4th and 8th Returns, 1st Briefing Train and the 120th Battery R.G.A. Ordinary routine and office duties.	M.P.
—do—	26/4		"	M.P.
—do—	27/4		"	M.P.
—do—	28/4		Obtained 10 days leave "urgent private affairs" and left for England	M.P.
—do—	29/4		" On leave	M.P.
—do—	30/4		"	M.P.

9.5.16.

R.A. Plunkett Major A.V.C.
A.D.V.S., 33rd Division.

WAR DIARY of Major R.A. Rennick R.A.M.C. ADVS, 33rd DIVN. for MAY, 1916.

Vol 7

INTELLIGENCE SUMMARY

Army Form C. 2118.

Place	Date 1916 MAY	Hour	Summary of Events and Information	Remarks and references to Appendices
BETHUNE	1st to 8th		In England on leave	N.O. N.O.
BETHUNE	9th		I arrived back in Bethune	
"	10th		Ordinary routine and office duties.	N.O.
"	11th		Inspected animals of C Battery, 167 Brigade, which on a whole show a slight improvement.	N.O.
"	12th		During Exam animal from 2nd Worcesters reacting to malleine test at Base. Last of all animals of this unit retested. Inspected B & C Batteries, 162 Brigade R.F.A. also Column of this Brigade.	N.O.
"	13th		Usual weekly conference of V.O's held at my office. Inspected animals of 33rd Divl. Ammunition Column. On the whole the animals are looking fairly well	N.O.
"	14th		Parade of animals of 115, 212th and 222nd Field Cos. R.E. and inspected animals of 2nd Worcesters re malleine test. RESULT NIL	N.O.
"	15th		Inspected horses of 166 Brigade R.F.A. except Ammunition Column.	N.O.

Army Form C. 2118.

WAR DIARY

INTELLIGENCE SUMMARY.

(Erase heading not required.)

Place	Date 1916	Hour	Summary of Events and Information	Remarks and references to Appendices
BETHUNE	MAY 16		Walked round the lines and inspected animals of Ammunition Column, 156 Brigade and H Battery, 162 Brigade and H Battery, 162 Brigade R.F.A.	
"	17		Visited stantings and inspected horses of Ammunition Column, 166 Brigade R.F.A.	
"	18		Examined the horses of No 2 Section, 1st Army Auxiliary Horse transport A.S.C. These animals although slightly improved since my previous inspection, are still in poor condition. 118th Heavy Battery arrives to replace 129th H.B. in 4+2nd H.A.G. 129th Battery moves to 2nd Div: area.	
"	19		Saw all the animals of 100th Infantry Brigade horsed. Their horses and mules are looking much better.	
"	20		Inspected animals of the newly arrived 118th Heavy Battery. Taking them altogether, they are rather a poor lot, and I found it necessary to evacuate a number Cases.	
"	21		Ordinary Routine and Office duties	

WAR DIARY
or
INTELLIGENCE SUMMARY.
(Erase heading not required.)

Army Form C. 2118.

Place	Date 1916	Hour	Summary of Events and Information	Remarks and references to Appendices
BETHUNE	22		Walked round the lines and inspected animals of 100th Brigade Machine Gun Company. Had an interview with O.C. and made a few inspections regarding the care of his animals.	M.O.
"	23		Ordinary routine office duties.	M.O.
"	24		Inspected a party of 81 surplus animals, from 4 to their departure by road to Calais. This aptness has been caused by the absorption of Artillery Brigade Ammunition Columns by the Divisional Ammunition Column. This arrangement has relieved three Sergeants A.V.C. which are now surplus, pending instructions from D.D.V.S.	M.O.
"	25		Inspected billets and animals of the 33rd Divisional Signal Company R.E. Condition of horses and mules is much improved.	M.O.
"	26		Conference with V.O.'s and ordinary routine and office duties.	M.O.

WAR DIARY
or
INTELLIGENCE SUMMARY.
(Erase heading not required.)

Army Form C. 2118.

Instructions regarding War Diaries and Intelligence Summaries are contained in F. S. Regs., Part II. and the Staff Manual respectively. Title pages will be prepared in manuscript.

Place	Date 1916	Hour	Summary of Events and Information	Remarks and references to Appendices
BETHUNE	MAY 27		Ordinary routine and office duties.	MP
"	28		Lines arrival of 164 Brigade R.F.A.	MP
"	29		Inspected, in their billets, all the animals of the 98th Infantry Brigade, except Machine Gun Company. Both horses and mules were looking well. Those of the 4th Suffolks in particular being particularly good.	MP
"	30		Inspected lines and animals of D/116 2. Animals very much improved, those of D Battery, 156 Brigade R.F.A. are rather from appearance, the losing condition.	MP
"	31		Walked round lines and inspected animals of A.T. Batteries, 156 Brigade R.F.A. Some of the half which there units have received entirely, have been very bad.	MP

W.R. Plunkitt Major A.V.C.
A.D.V.S., 33rd Div:

1577 Wt. W10791/1773 500,000 1/15 D. D. & L. A.D.S.S./Forms/C. 2118.

WAR DIARY of Major R.A. Plunkett ADVS 33rd Divn: Army Form C. 2118.
for June 1916 **VOL 8**

INTELLIGENCE SUMMARY.
(Erase heading not required.)

Place	Date	Hour	Summary of Events and Information	Remarks and references to Appendices
BÉTHUNE	1916 June 1		Parades animals and inspected lines of B Echelon, 33rd Divisional Ammunition Column. Animals are much improved, but the watering arrangements need improvement.	ADMS
"	2		Lines and animals of 100th Brigade Machine Gun Company. Mules are in poor condition. Referred to D.H.Q. the desirability of this unit having a transport officer which does not after the formed form the transport establishment laid down. In conjunction with V.O. to supplement the newly arrived 38th Heavy Battery R.G.A. animals. Conference of V.O's	ADMS
"	3		Inspected animals of 38th Heavy Battery under Fort. No objections, also had a journey of animals of C. Battery 166 Brigade R.F.A. which are looking fairly well.	ADMS

WAR DIARY

of

INTELLIGENCE SUMMARY.

Army Form C. 2118.

of Army, 33rd Division June continued

Place	Date 1916	Hour	Summary of Events and Information	Remarks and references to Appendices
BETHUNE	June 4		Attended conference of A.D's.M.S. with D.D.M.S. at 1st Army Headquarters.	M.O.
"	5		Ordinary routine and office duties.	M.O.
"	6		Meetings Officers of recently arrived 98th Brigade M.G. Company. Inspected vinb animals of 118th Battery R.G.A.	M.O.
"	7		" " No 2 Section, 33rd Bn. also animals of 98th Bde. M.G. Co. under test. No reaction.	M.O.
"	8		Inspected animals of 100th Bde: M.G. Co. under mallein test. No reaction.	M.O.

WAR DIARY of Major R A Plunkett R.V.C. DADVS, 33rd Divn.

Army Form C. 2118.

INTELLIGENCE SUMMARY.
(Erase heading not required.)

for June, 1916 (continued)

Place	Date 1916	Hour	Summary of Events and Information	Remarks and references to Appendices
	9		Conference of V.O's. — Ordinary routine duties.	W.D.R.
	10		Had a parade of all animals of 19th Infantry Brigade except 20th Royal Fusiliers. General condition good.	W.D.R.
	11		Ordinary routine duties.	W.D.R.
	12		In company with ADVS 16th and 39th Divisions accompanied the DDVS on visit to Base Hospital Abbeville to inspect method of working.	W.D.R.
	13		Inspected all A.V.C. Sergeants attached Batteries and Infantry Brigades, in full marching order, examined their Case Books and inspected equipment. The first parade into which the methylated spirit flask fits (in the famous Mullet) is satisfactory as it sticks to the flask	W.D.R.

WAR DIARY of ADVS 33rd Division

June 1916 Continued

INTELLIGENCE SUMMARY

Place	Date 1916	Hour	Summary of Events and Information	Remarks and references to Appendices
BETHUNE	June 13		(Continued) A number of the bucks have been damaged in the attempt to get them out of the first movement. ~~...~~ After the female infected the Sarsaparilla on the "Case of horses and chemux" thus each a sample of the Castor oil team in order that they may be able to paint the V.O's in the detection, showed any of those horses come up.	11.30 am
	14	11.30	Inspected a number of O.C. Cases @ M.V.S. An infectedly getting complaints from units that they are often getting loaves of dirty oats and it is usually impossible that contractors having to Sack not being marked	11.30
	15		Animals & lives of B.C. Batteries 164 Brigade R.F.A.	11.45

WAR DIARY of A.D.V.S., 33rd Divn. for June, 1916

INTELLIGENCE SUMMARY.
(Erase heading not required.)

Army Form C. 2118.

Instructions regarding War Diaries and Intelligence Summaries are contained in F. S. Regs., Part II. and the Staff Manual respectively. Title pages will be prepared in manuscript.

Place	Date 1916	Hour	Summary of Events and Information	Remarks and references to Appendices
BETHUNE	June 16		Visited lines and inspected animals of 20th Royal Fusiliers and No 3 Section, 33rd D.A.C.	M.O?
"	17		Animals of No 1 Section, 33rd D.A.C. paraded for my inspection	M.O?
"	18		Veterinary care of animals of D. Battery, 179 and C Battery, 186 Brigade R.F.A. is transferred from 39th to this Division.	M.O?
"	19		Lines & animals of B + C Batteries, 156 Brigade R.F.A. inspected	M.O?
"	20		Parade of animals of D/162 which are much improved since my last inspection	M.O?

Army Form C. 2118.

WAR DIARY of A.D.V.S., 33rd Divn;
INTELLIGENCE SUMMARY.
(Erase heading not required.)

for June, 1916.

Instructions regarding War Diaries and Intelligence Summaries are contained in F. S. Regs., Part II. and the Staff Manual respectively. Title pages will be prepared in manuscript.

Place	Date 1916	Hour	Summary of Events and Information	Remarks and references to Appendices
BETHUNE	June 21		Inspected animals of No 2 Section, 1st Army Auxiliary Horse Transport, A.S.C. and 101st Field Ambulance. The animals of former unit, though slightly improved since last inspection are still in an unsatisfactory condition, and I found it necessary to put 12 fifteen spare for a period of rest. The Ambulance animals were looking well.	N.R.
"	22		Parade of animals of 1/6 South Riflers rendered complete merging with this Battn. and the 1/5 forming one composite Battalion.	N.R.
"	23		Ordinary routine duties. Conference of V.O's.	N.R.
"	24		Lines and animals of B. and D. Batteries, 156 Brigade inspected.	N.R.

T2134. Wt. W708—776. 500000. 4/15. Sir J. C. & S.

Army Form C. 2118.

WAR DIARY of A.D.V.S, 33rd Divn. INTELLIGENCE SUMMARY. for June, 1916

(Erase heading not required.)

Instructions regarding War Diaries and Intelligence Summaries are contained in F. S. Regs., Part II. and the Staff Manual respectively. Title pages will be prepared in manuscript.

Place	Date 1916	Hour	Summary of Events and Information	Remarks and references to Appendices
BETHUNE	June 25		Inspected animals of D.H.Q. Staff, including all details.	M.R.
"	26		A number of surplus animals from R.F.A. handed in for my inspection at VENDIN church.	M.R.
"	27		Walked round lines. Inspected animals of D.R. Battery 162 Brigade R.F.A. The animals have much improved and are looking well.	M.R.
"	28		Ordinary routine duties	M.R.
"	29		Walked round lines. Inspected animals of following Batteries:- D/166, D/149, A and C 166 Brigades R.F.A.	M.R.
"	30		Ordinary routine duties	M.R.

H.A. Plumbett Major A.V.C.
A.D.V.S, 33rd Divn.

33 July
Army Form C. 2118.

WAR DIARY of Major R.A. Plunkett, A.V.C.
INTELLIGENCE SUMMARY. A.D.V.S, 33rd Division
for July, 1916

(Erase heading not required.)

Place	Date	Hour	Summary of Events and Information	Remarks and references to Appendices
BETHUNE	1916 July 1		Veterinary routine and office duties.	N.B.O.
—"—	2		Walked round lines and inspected animals of No 2 Section D.A.C. Animals are in fairly good condition and certainly improved since I last inspected them.	N.B.O.
—"—	3		Veterinary routine and office duties.	N.B.O.
—"—	4		Parade of animals of No 3 Section D.A.C. and picked out a few debilitated animals for evacuation.	N.B.O.
—"—	5		Inspected animals of Nos 1 and 4 Sections D.A.C. and 162 Brigade R.F.A. General condition good, shoeing satisfactory.	N.B.O.
—"—	6		Inspected animals of recently arrived Signal Section at CHOQUES. Animals, which were under mallein test, showed no reaction.	N.B.O.

WAR DIARY of Major R.A. Pennett, A.V.C.
A.D.V.S. 33rd Division. B.E.F. for July, 1916

Army Form C. 2118.

INTELLIGENCE SUMMARY.
(Erase heading not required.)

Instructions regarding War Diaries and Intelligence Summaries are contained in F. S. Regs., Part II. and the Staff Manual respectively. Title pages will be prepared in manuscript.

Place	Date 1916	Hour	Summary of Events and Information	Remarks and references to Appendices
TREUX	July 15		Left TREUX for MÉAULTE. Advanced Dressing Station for M.V.S. U.D.P. established at BECORDEL.	
MÉAULTE	16		Inspected water supply for R.V.A. animals at BECORDEL. The supply seems quite inadequate, but on enquiring I learn that it is only a temporary distribution which will be adjusted immediately. A large number of animals of 166 Brigade were caught by hostile shell fire whilst taking ammunition to the guns. Inspected watering arrangements in Fricourt Mametz Road.	N.A.P.
"	17		Visited R.V.A. wagon lines at BECORDEL, also Advanced Dressing Station of M.V.S. & a few other units in vicinity. Watering & shoeing arrangements satisfactory.	N.A.P.
"	18		Watered troughs fixed up in FRICOURT wood where watered cavalry had hitherto been inadequate. Inspected animals of 11th, 212th T222nd	N.A.P.

WAR DIARY of Major R.A. Plunkett M.V.C.
A.D.V.S. 33rd Division.
B.E.F. for July, 1916

Army Form C. 2118.

INTELLIGENCE SUMMARY.
(Erase heading not required.)

Place	Date	Hour	Summary of Events and Information	Remarks and references to Appendices
BETHUNE	1916 July 7		Ordinary routine duties. Moving orders received.	M.O.
"	8		Left Bethune [struck through] and [struck through] BELLOY-sur-SOMME on the 9th, arrived	M.O.
BELLOY	10		Looking round animals of units in vicinity	M.O.
"	11		Left BELLOY for CORBIE where we arrived same evening	M.O.
CORBIE	12		Left CORBIE for TREUX where we arrived same evening	M.O.
TREUX	13		Visited 156, 162, 166, 167 T.M.B. who were in vicinity and conferred with each V.O. Artillery moved away same night.	M.O.
"	14		Visited MÉAULTE to select billet for Mobile Section	M.O.

WAR DIARY of Major R.A. Pennhett, A.V.C.
ADVV, 33rd Divn.,
B.E.F. for July 1916

Army Form C. 2118.

INTELLIGENCE SUMMARY.
(Erase heading not required.)

Place	Date 1916	Hour	Summary of Events and Information	Remarks and references to Appendices
MÉAULTE	July 18		(Continued) Field Cos. R.E. 3 Battns. of 156 Brigade R.F.A. and 100th Machine Gun Company. All animals looking well except but mentioned.	WAR.
"	19		Visited M.V.S. Advanced Collecting Station at BECORDEL.	WAR.
"	20		During the week ending on this date there has been a large number of casualties amongst R.F.A. animals. The 166 Brigade had the greatest number with 29 either killed by or destroyed suffering from shrapnel wounds. Two or three days ago I made representations to D.H.Q. that these wagon lines be moved to a less exposed position. Moved from MÉAULTE village into another ALBERT-BRAY road about 1 Km from ALBERT.	WAR.
"	21		Inspected animals of A/167 which are not looking at all well though the feeding & watering arrangements appear to be satisfactory.	WAR.

Army Form C. 2118.

WAR DIARY of Major R.A. Plunkett A.V.C. asgn 33rd Divn B.E.F. for July, 1916

INTELLIGENCE SUMMARY.
(Erase heading not required.)

Instructions regarding War Diaries and Intelligence Summaries are contained in F.S. Regs., Part II. and the Staff Manual respectively. Title pages will be prepared in manuscript.

Place	Date 1916	Hour	Summary of Events and Information	Remarks and references to Appendices
CAMP NEAR NEAULTE	July 2		Inspected animals of 162 Brigade R.F.A., A.B., C.D Batteries took well, but Wh. initial ammunition in C. The in poor condition and picked out 3 for convalescent. Moved to RIBEMONT. Office established at LA MAIRIE.	Lieut W.M?
RIBEMONT	3		Entrainmnt line animals of 19, 99, 170 Field Ambulances and 18th Middlesex three of entire unit are looking exceptionally well. Moved from Ribemont ETREUX. Office opened at Ferme of Martin's CHATEAU. Notices received from 8 Bonneed punishing not immediately that Lime transport pickitting near new pertine, owing to large quantities of arsenic which have recently been removed from this Canal	R.M.? N.S.?
TREUX	4		Inspected animals of 33rd Signal Coy. R.E.	N.R.?

Army Form C. 2118.

WAR DIARY of Major R.A. Pennett, AVC.
~~INTELLIGENCE SUMMARY.~~
RVM/J 33rd Division, BEF for July, 1916.
(Erase heading not required.)

Instructions regarding War Diaries and Intelligence Summaries are contained in F.S. Regs., Part II. and the Staff Manual respectively. Title pages will be prepared in manuscript.

Place	Date 1916	Hour	Summary of Events and Information	Remarks and references to Appendices
TREUX	July 25		Moved from TREUX to D 29 C.3.3., near camps near BUIRE.	Map.
CAMP 20	26		Visited 162 Brigade R.F.A. and No 1 and 2 Sections D.A.C. Watering arrangements satisfactory, but amount of No 2 Section are very much overcrowded on lines, which I suggested should be changed.	
" "	27		Inspected animals of 98th Infantry Brigade.	Map.
" "	28		" a engagement of remounts at MERICOURT. Attended conference of A.D.V.S. of 4th Army Headquarters	Map.
"	29		Inspected Mobile Section & Advanced Collecting Station	M.D.D.
"	30		" animals of 83rd Brig. Co R.E. Great improvement noted	d.d.
"	31		Visited BECORDEL. Experimented with each V.O. of R.F.A. Brigade	Map.

WAR DIARY of Major R.A. Plunkett. A.V.C. Army Form C. 2118
A.D.V.S. 33rd Divn

INTELLIGENCE SUMMARY

Vol 10

Place	Date	Hour	Summary of Events and Information	Remarks and references to Appendices
Buire	Aug 1		Inspected the Animals, lines, and forage of the 100th Bde. Hay coming up is of poor quality. Temporary dislocation of water supply at Becourt Wood.	W.D.^o
"	" 2		Inspected 6 r.B. Batteries of 167 Bde and No 3 Section D.A.C. A percentage of the hay coming up is poor, but the present issue of oats is of very good quality.	W.D.^o
"	" 3		Inspected 25 remounts on arrival at railhead, general condition of animals fair.	W.D.^o
"	" 4		Inspected the animals and lines of 162 and 166 Bde R.F.A. with exception of 2 Batteries both Brigades are in good condition. Watering arrangements good.	W.D.^o
"	" 5		Inspected 100th Infantry Brigade r M.G. Company and 16th Middlesex Pioneers.	W.D.^o
"	" 6		Moved from BUIRE to ALBERT-BRAY Road.	W.D.^o
ALBERT Road	" 7		Ordinary routine and office duties. 6 Animals killed and 4 wounded cm 167 Brigade while taking ammunition up to the guns.	W.D.^o

WAR DIARY of Major R.O. Plunkett A.V.C. Army Form C. 2118
or A.D.V.S. 33rd Division
INTELLIGENCE SUMMARY

(Erase heading not required.)

Instructions regarding War Diaries and Intelligence Summaries are contained in F.S. Regs., Part II. and the Staff Manual respectively. Title Pages will be prepared in manuscript.

Place	Date	Hour	Summary of Events and Information	Remarks and references to Appendices
ALBERT Roadbg 8.	Aug 8		Inspected animals and lines of 212 Field Company Royal Engineers.	MVO
"	" 9		Inspected animals of 24th Batt. Manchester Pioneers (attached)	MVO
"	" 10		Inspected animals of A Battery 167 Bde and 54 Coy R.E. (attached) shoeing of both batteries good.	MVO
"	" 11		Ordinary routine and office duties.	MVO
"	" 12		Inspected 156 & 167 Bde's R.F.A. in rest area, with exception of one Battery, both Brigades are in good condition	MVO
"	" 13		Inspected remounts on arrival at railhead, general condition of animals unsatisfactory.	MVO
"	" 14		Inspected C. Battery 156 Bde & B. Battery 167 Brigade, and selected several thin horses suffering from debility for evacuation	MVO
"	" 15		Inspected the animals of 166 Bde R.F.A., and selected several thin horses suffering from debility for evacuation. also inspected the sick horses for evacuation at M.V.S	MVO
"	" 16.		Inspected the animals of 162 Bde R.F.A, also attended conference of A.D.s V.S at No 12 M.V.S. MERICOURT.	MVO

WAR DIARY
or
INTELLIGENCE SUMMARY

(Erase heading not required.)

Army Form C. 2118

Place	Date	Hour	Summary of Events and Information	Remarks and references to Appendices
ALBERT ROAD	Aug 17		Parade of A.V.C. Sergeants at M.V.S with Veterinary Wallets, for my inspection. Inspected the animals of No 2 Section D.A.C. also inspected sick animals for evacuation at M.V.S.	M.V?
"	" 18		Inspected the fodder and hay issued to the 166 Bde. R.F.A.	M.V?
"	" 19		Inspected horses, fodder and lines of the 192nd Infantry Brigade	M.V?
"	" 20		Inspected all evacuation cases at M.V.S	M.V?
"	" 21		Inspection of all evacuation cases at railhead, their food supply, and watering arrangements enquired into, for journey, suggested to D.H.Q. regarding the erection of a trough at railhead so that horses entraining and detraining may be watered.	M.V?
"	" 22		Inspected No 1 Section. D.A.C. condition of animals satisfactory	M.V?
"	" 23		Inspected the animals of D Battery 162 Brigade, also inspected sick horses at M.V.S for evacuation. Reported to Headquarters C. the unsuitability of R.E. waggon lines, owing to shell fire.	M.V?
"	" 24		Ordinary routine and office duties.	M.V?

WAR DIARY of Major R.A. Plunkett. A.V. Army Form C. 2118
A.D.V.S. 33rd Divn
INTELLIGENCE SUMMARY

(Erase heading not required.)

Place	Date	Hour	Summary of Events and Information	Remarks and references to Appendices
ALBERT. road	Aug 25		Inspected the animals of 3 Company's R.E.'s and 19th Infantry Brigade	W.P.
"	" 26		Inspected the animals of 2 Batteries of 167 Bde in rest area, also attended the entraining of evacuation cases at railhead.	W.P.
"	" 27		Ordinary routine and office duties	W.P.
"	" 28		Inspection of remounts on arrival at railhead.	W.P.
"	" 29		Inspected the animals and lines of 156 Bde. R.F.A.	W.P.
"	" 30		Inspected the animals of 18th Middlesex Pioneers, also inspected all sick horses at M.V.S for evacuation.	W.P.
"	" 31		Moved from ALBERT-BRAY road to VILLERS-BOCAGE.	W.P.

WAR DIARY of Major R.A. Plunkett A.V.C.
A.D.V.S. 33rd Div'n

Army Form C. 2118.

or

INTELLIGENCE SUMMARY.

(Erase heading not required.)

Vol II

Place	Date	Hour	Summary of Events and Information	Remarks and references to Appendices
Villers-Brocage	Sept 1		Ordinary routine and office duties	
Bernaville	" 2		Left Villers-Brocage for Bernaville, office at Ercle-de-Garcon.	M.O.
"	" 3		Ordinary routine and office duties	M.O.
Trochen-le-Grand	" 4		Left Bernaville for Trochen-le-Grand, office at Ercle-de-Garcon.	M.O.
Hers	" 5		Left Trochen-le-Grand for Hers, office at Au-gres-Silent. Inspected the animals and lines of 1st Middlesex.	M.O.
"	" 6		Reported my arrival into this area, to D.D.V.S. at 3rd Army Headquarters.	M.O.
"	" 7		Inspected the animals of 100th M.G. bty. and 4 Coy Lowri, watering arrangements insufficient, in a portion of this area, some of the animals having to go 2 kilometres, for the supply	M.O.
"	" 8		Inspected all evacuation cases at rail head.	M.O.
Pas	" 9		Left Hers for Pas, office at 159 La-Place.	M.O.
"	" 10		Ordinary routine and office duties.	M.O.
"	" 11		Inspected the animals and lines of 11th and 212 Field Coy R.E.	M.O.
"	" 12		Inspected the animals of 100th Infantry Brigade, shoeing good, watering arrangements favourable	M.O.

WAR DIARY of Major R.A. Plunkett. A.V.C.
Y.D.O./8 33rd Division
INTELLIGENCE SUMMARY.

Army Form C. 2118.

(Erase heading not required.)

Place	Date	Hour	Summary of Events and Information	Remarks and references to Appendices
Pas	Sep/13		Inspected the animals and lines of the 19th Infantry Brigade.	
"	" 14		Inspected the animals and lines of 162 Bde, 116 Bde and B. Battery 156 Bde R.F.A., selected several thin horses, suffering from debility, for evacuation.	1 ap.
"	" 15		Inspection of horses and lines of No 4 Section D.A.C.	
"	" 16		Inspected the animals of 33rd Signal Coy R.E.	
"	" 17		Ordinary routine and office duties.	
"	" 18		Inspected all sick horses for evacuation at M.V.S.	
"	" 19		Inspected the animals of 19th - 98th Infantry Brigades, and 156 Bde R.F.A.	1 ap.
"	" 20		Inspected the animals and lines of 162 Bde R.F.A.	
"	" 21		Inspection of all sick horses for evacuation at M.V.S.	
Henu	" 22		Left Pas for Henu, office at Mairie House. Inspected 99, 101st Field Ambulance and Head quarters Coy Train	
"	" 23		Inspected all sick horses for evacuation at M.V.S.	
"	" 24		Inspected the animals of 3rd Pontoon Park, 6 Coy 3rd Labour Battalion, 141st Coy Army Troops R.E., and 3rd Field Survey Coy R.E. (attached)	1 ap.
"	" 25		Inspected the animals of 156 - 162 - 166 Bde R.F.A. and No 1 - 2 v 3 Sections D.A.C.	

WAR DIARY of Major R. O. Plunkett A.V.C
A.D.V.S 33rd Division   Army Form C. 2118.

INTELLIGENCE SUMMARY.
(Erase heading not required.)

Place	Date	Hour	Summary of Events and Information	Remarks and references to Appendices
Hem	Sept/26		Inspected the animals of 110th M.G. Coy, 131st M.G. Coy (attached) and 222 Coy R.E	nil
"	" 27		Inspected the animals of 132 Coy. army troops R.E	nil
"	" 28		Inspection of all Units by D.D.V.S	nil
"	" 29		Ordinary routine and office duties	nil
Doullens	" 30		Left Hem for Doullens, office at I.22	nil

Instructions regarding War Diaries and Intelligence
Summaries are contained in F. S. Regs., Part II.
and the Staff Manual respectively. Title pages
will be prepared in manuscript.

Army Form C. 2118.

WAR DIARY of Major R.O. Plunkett, AVC
O.D.O/S 32nd Division
—of—
INTELLIGENCE SUMMARY.

Vol 12

(Erase heading not required.)

Place	Date	Hour	Summary of Events and Information	Remarks and references to Appendices
Doullens	1-10-16		Inspected the animals and lines of the 95th Infantry Brigade. Watering arrangements satisfactory	11 NP
"	2-10-16		Inspected the animals of 33rd Signal Coy R.E.	11 NP
"	3-10-16		Inspected the animals and lines of the 11th Field Coy R.E. Condition of animals good.	11 NP
"	4-10-16		Ordinary routine and office duties.	11 NP
"	5-10-16		Inspected the animals and lines of the 96th Infantry Brigade	11 NP
"	6-10-16		Inspected the animals of 32nd Reserve Park (attached). Shoeing and watering arrangements satisfactory	11 NP
"	7-10-16		Inspected the animals and lines of 100th Infantry Brigade. Watering arrangements favourable	11 NP
"	8-10-16		Inspected the animals and lines of the 21st Royal Fusiliers.	11 NP
"	9-10-16		Ordinary routine and office duties	11 NP
"	11-10-16		Obtained 9 days leave and proceeded to England.	11 NP
Corbie	19-10-16		Returned off leave. Left Doullens for Corbie. Office at "The College".	11 NP
"	20-10-16		Ordinary routine and office duties.	11 NP
"	21-10-16		Moved from Corbie to Treux	11 NP

T.J.134. Wt. W708—776. 500000. 4/15. Sir J. C. & S.

Army Form C. 2118.

WAR DIARY of Major. R.A. Plunkett. R.C.
A.D.V.S 23rd Division

INTELLIGENCE SUMMARY.
(Erase heading not required.)

Instructions regarding War Diaries and Intelligence Summaries are contained in F. S. Regs., Part II. and the Staff Manual respectively. Title pages will be prepared in manuscript.

Place	Date	Hour	Summary of Events and Information	Remarks and references to Appendices
Front	22-10-16		Moved from Front to F.21-B Central.	N.W.R.
F.21.B Central	23-10-16		Inspected new location for M.V.S, and located attached units	N.W.R.
"	24-10-16		Inspected the animals and lines of 1947 100th Infantry Brigades	N.W.R.
"	25-10-16		Moved from F.21-B Central to A.2.d.9.7.	N.W.R.
A.2.d.9.7	26-10-16		Inspected the animals of 18th Middlesex and 33rd Signal Coy R.E.	N.W.R.
"	27-10-16		Inspected animals and lines of 99th Field Ambulance	N.W.R.
"	28-10-16		Inspected the animals of 56th Divisional Artillery (attached)	N.W.R.
"	29-10-16		Selected new location for M.V.S. and visited advanced Headquarters	N.W.R.
"	30-10-16		Inspected the 4th Divisional Artillery (attached) and sent horses for evacuation	N.W.R.
"	31-10-16		Visited the D.D.V.S. on duty.	N.W.R.

WAR DIARY of Major R.O. Plunkett. A.V.C.
A.D.V.S. 33rd Divn.

Vol 13

Army Form C. 2118.

WAR DIARY
or
INTELLIGENCE SUMMARY.
(Erase heading not required.)

Instructions regarding War Diaries and Intelligence Summaries are contained in F. S. Regs., Part II. and the Staff Manual respectively. Title pages will be prepared in manuscript.

Place	Date	Hour	Summary of Events and Information	Remarks and references to Appendices
A2 d.9.7	Nov. 1.16		Inspected all sick animals for evacuation at M.V.S. Visited Advanced Head-quarters.	M.O?
"	2.16		Inspected the animals and lines of the 19th Infantry Brigade and Machine gun Coy. general condition of animals satisfactory.	
"	3.16		Inspected the animals and lines of 19th and 99th field ambulances, also Mules for casting in 6th Division	
"	4.16		Inspected the animals at Advanced Headquarters, 33rd Signal Coy R.E. and 1st Middlesex Pioneers.	M.S?
"	5.16		Inspected the animals and lines of No.4 Sect D.A.C, 212th Field Coy R.E. and 2nd Argyle & Sutherlands. Suggestions how horses shoes may be prevented from falling off, circulated to all Veterinary Officers.	
"	6.16		Inspected the animals and lines of 157th Battery, 32nd Brigade.	M.S?
"	7.16		Visited Advanced Veterinary Post, and assisted in saving two horses, which had fallen into shell holes. Inspected the animals and lines of No.4 Coy Train; general condition of animals good.	
"	8.16		Moved from A.2.d.9.7 to Treux.	

Army Form C. 2118.

WAR DIARY of Major R.A. Plunkett A.V.C.
A.D.V.S. 33rd Div'n

INTELLIGENCE SUMMARY.

(Erase heading not required.)

Instructions regarding War Diaries and Intelligence Summaries are contained in F. S. Regs., Part II. and the Staff Manual respectively. Title pages will be prepared in manuscript.

Place	Date	Hour	Summary of Events and Information	Remarks and references to Appendices
Treux	9.1.16		Ordinary routine and office duties.	4 W.D.
"	10.16		Moved from Treux to Thelincourt. Office at Glas Hotel-de-ville.	4 W.D.
Hallincourt	11.16		Inspection of all animals at M.V.S.	4 W.D.
"	12.16		Inspected the animals of Head-quarters Divnl. Train, condition of animals good.	4 W.D.
"	13.16		Inspected the animals and lines of 5th Scottish, 2nd Royal Welsh Fusiliers, and No. 3 Coy. Train, condition of all animals satisfactory.	4 W.D.
"	13.16		Inspected the animals of 20th Royal Fusiliers, 1st Cameronians, and 19th Machine Gun Coy. The animals of the 20th R.F. show signs of fatigue, the latter are in excellent condition.	4 W.D.
"	15.16		Inspected the animals of No. 1 Sect. D.A.C. general condition of animals satisfactory.	4 W.D.
"	15.16		Inspected all such animals for evacuation at M.V.S.	4 W.D.
"	16.16		Inspected the animals of 96th I. Bde. and 99th Field ambulance. Horses are in excellent condition. Grooming of 1st Middlesex very good.	4 W.D.
"	17.16		Inspected the animals of B.L. Cable Section (attached.	4 W.D.
"	18.16		Inspected the animals of 98th Machine Gun Coy and No.1 Coy. Train.	4 W.D.
"	19.16			

Army Form C. 2118.

WAR DIARY of Major R.A. Stuart, RAMC
O Does 33rd Divn.

INTELLIGENCE SUMMARY.
(Erase heading not required.)

Instructions regarding War Diaries and Intelligence Summaries are contained in F. S. Regs., Part II. and the Staff Manual respectively. Title pages will be prepared in manuscript.

Place	Date	Hour	Summary of Events and Information	Remarks and references to Appendices
Mallurscourt	9/6/16 21.16		Took over position and office duties. Inspected the animals of 1st Queens and N.L.I. condition of animals good.	Q.M?
"	22.16		Inspected ground suitable for horse lines for Artillery.	A.V?
"	23.16		Inspected the animals of F.R.E. and Machine gun Cy. grooming satisfactory. Condition of animals good.	N.V?
"	24.16		Inspected the animals of 9th gr. 1st & 2nd, 4th Suffolks, 10/1st Middx. and 11/0. and N? 2 Cy Train. The animals of the Infantry are on satisfactory condition. Condition of animals as N? 2 of Train excellent.	N.V?
"	25.16		Inspected the animals of 2nd O.V.S.H. Condition of animals satisfactory. Grooming fair. Made arrangements with R.A. to inspect Brigades.	N.V?
"	26.16		Inspected the animals of 150 Field Cy R6. Condition of animals good.	A.V?
"	27.16		Inspected the animals of N? 1 & 3 Sections D.A.C. Condition of animals for N? 1 sect. N.V? satisfactory, animals of N? 3 sect very good. Moving up to the	
"	28.16		Inspected of Remounts on arrival at Milhnead, also inspected animals of 1/1st Middlesex Remount. Condition of animals satisfactory.	N.V?
"	29.16		Inspected the animals of 156 O.A.R.H. General condition of animals satisfactory.	N.V?
"	30.16		Inspected the animals of 1st Fd Cy R.E. 222 & Sig C6, & N? 2 sect. D.A.C. Condition of all animals satisfactory.	N.V?

Army Form C. 2118.

WAR DIARY of Major R.A. Plunkett. AVC
A.D.V.S. 33rd Division
INTELLIGENCE SUMMARY.
(Erase heading not required.)

Vol 14

Instructions regarding War Diaries and Intelligence Summaries are contained in F.S. Regs., Part II. and the Staff Manual respectively. Title pages will be prepared in manuscript.

Place	Date	Hour	Summary of Events and Information	Remarks and references to Appendices
HALLENCOURT	1916 Dec 1		Inspected the animals and lines of 162 Brigade R.F.A. General condition of all animals satisfactory. Shoeing up to date.	M.W.O.
"	" 2		Inspected all sick animals for evacuation at 33rd Mobile Veterinary Section.	M.W.O. M.W.O.
"	" 3		Parade of AVC Sergeants attached 33rd Division, for my inspection. Veterinary Wallets and cast boots.	M.W.O.
"	" 4		Inspected the animals and lines of 33rd Signal Coy R.E. Grooming of all horses satisfactory.	M.W.O.
"	" 5		Moved from Hallencourt to Albert.	M.W.O.
ALBERT	" 6		Inspected the animals of Divisional Headquarters.	M.W.O.
"	" 7		Inspected animals and lines of 1st Kings. Grooming and shoeing satisfactory.	M.W.O.
"	" 8		Inspected animals and lines of No. 4 Coy Train. Condition of animals good. Shoeing up to date.	M.W.O.
"	" 9		Inspected four battalions of 98th Infantry Brigade, and 101st Field Ambulance.	M.W.O.
"	" 10		Ordinary routine and office duties.	M.W.O.

Army Form C. 2118.

War Diary of Major R.A. Shuttock
A.D.V.S. 33rd Divn.

WAR DIARY
INTELLIGENCE SUMMARY.
(Erase heading not required.)

Instructions regarding War Diaries and Intelligence Summaries are contained in F.S. Regs., Part II. and the Staff Manual respectively. Title pages will be prepared in manuscript.

Place	Date	Hour	Summary of Events and Information	Remarks and references to Appendices
	1916			
ALBERT	Dec 11		Visited Mauvres Ravine, and inspected all animals in Watana. Located and inspected lines of 100th Infantry Brigade at Camp 21. Inspected animals and lines of 222 Coy R.E.	W.R.
"	12		Inspected animals and lines of 18th Middlesex Pioneers. General condition of all animals satisfactory.	W.R.
"	13		Arranged for increase in water supply for animals at Camp 21. Inspected animals and lines of No 14 Section D.A.C.	W.R.
"	14		Inspected the animals of 162 Brigade R.F.A. and selected several thin horses suffering from debility, for evacuation.	W.R.
"	15		Moved from Albert to L16.d.1.9.	W.R.
L16.d.1.9.	16		Inspected A and B. batteries 156 Brigade R.F.A. Condition of animals fair.	W.R.
"	17		Inspected C and D. batteries 156 Brigade R.F.A. also inspected the strong of their animals	W.R.
"	18		Inspected 95th Bde Headquarters horses and M.G. Coy. General condition of all animals satisfactory. Inspected 212nd F.Coy R.E. grooming unsatisfactory	W.R.

WAR DIARY of Major R.A. Plunkett A.V.C. A.D.V.S. 33rd Divn

INTELLIGENCE SUMMARY

Army Form C. 2118.

(Erase heading not required.)

Instructions regarding War Diaries and Intelligence Summaries are contained in F.S. Regs., Part II. and the Staff Manual respectively. Title pages will be prepared in manuscript.

Place	Date	Hour	Summary of Events and Information	Remarks and references to Appendices
	1916			
L.16.d.1.9	Dec 19		Inspected animals of Group 18 & 34 R.G.A. General condition of all animals satisfactory. Shoeing up to date.	M.A.O.
"	" 20		Inspected animals and kits of No.1 and 2 Sections D.A.C. and selected several thin horses, suffering from Debility, to be sent to M.V.S.	M.A.O.
"	" 21		Inspected all animals at G.R.O. Headquarters. Inspected all sick animals for execution at M.V.S.	M.A.O.
"	" 22		Inspected the animals of 162 Bde R.F.A. Condition of animals fair.	
"	" 23		Attended conference at Army Head-quarters.	
"	" 24		Inspected animals of L.18 and No.1 Section D.A.C. All animals being carefully examined for skin diseases.	M.A.O.
"	" 25		Inspected the animals of 162 Bde R.F.A. Condition of animals satisfactory.	
"	" 26		Visited nuisances, to close light to M.S. Made veterinary inspection.	
"	" 27		Ordinary routine and office duties.	
"	" 28		Moved from L.16.d.1.9 to Derry. Office at 38° Fee Nauves.	
LONG	" 29		Inspected all animals of No.13 Section D.A.C. outbreak of Mays noted	
	" 30		" " " "	

WAR DIARY of Major R.A. Plunkett ARC
a.D.V.S. 33rd Divn

Army Form C. 2118.

Instructions regarding War Diaries and Intelligence Summaries are contained in F. S. Regs., Part II. and the Staff Manual respectively. Title pages will be prepared in manuscript.

INTELLIGENCE SUMMARY.
(Erase heading not required.)

Place	Date	Hour	Summary of Events and Information	Remarks and references to Appendices
LONG	1916 Dec 31		Inspected all animals of Divisional Headquarters, 33rd Signal Coy. R.E. 1st Middlesex Pioneers, and M.M.P. General condition of all animals satisfactory. Shoeing good.	M.P. Major ARC a.D.V.S. 33 Divn

Army Form C. 2118.

WAR DIARY of Major R.A. Plunkett AVC
or
INTELLIGENCE SUMMARY.
A.D.V.S. 33 Division

(Erase heading not required.)

Nov 1/5

Place	Date	Hour	Summary of Events and Information	Remarks and references to Appendices
LONG	Nov 1		Inspected the animals and lines of 2nd Royal Welsh Fusiliers and 5th Scottish Rifles. Condition of animals satisfactory. Shoeing up to date.	
"	2		Inspected animals of 1st Cameronians, 19th machine gun Coy and No 3 Coy Train. Condition of animals fair.	
"	3		Inspected animals of 20th Royal Fusiliers, No 2 Coy Train, and 11th Field Coy R.E. Condition of animals good. Shoeing and grooming satisfactory. Inspected animals of 99th, 101st Field Ambulances. also inspected the watering arrangements in this area.	
"	4		Individual examination of all horses in No 3 Coy Train for symptoms of Stomatitis, also inspected watering arrangements in this unit. Attended conference at Fourth Army Headquarters.	
"	5			
"	6		Inspected animals of 98th Infantry Brigade and No 2 Coy Train. Condition of all animals satisfactory.	
"	7		Lectured to "Transport Officers, Senior N.C.O's" Farriers, and Sergeants a&c. on "The minor clinical symptoms of the following horse epidemics". Sancoptic Mange, Contagious Stomatitis, Septic Cellulitis. So as to detect in the early	

Army Form C. 2118.

WAR DIARY of Major R.O. Plunkett. A.V.C.
A.D.V.S, 33 Div?
INTELLIGENCE SUMMARY.
(Erase heading not required.)

Instructions regarding War Diaries and Intelligence Summaries are contained in F. S. Regs, Part II. and the Staff Manual respectively. Title pages will be prepared in manuscript.

Place	Date	Hour	Summary of Events and Information	Remarks and references to Appendices
LONG	Jan 7.		Stages these diseases, and hereby prevent disease becoming general throughout units. Inspected Remounts on arrival at rail head. Condition of animals fair. Individually examined all horses in No 3 Coy Train for symptoms of Stomatitis.	✓
"	" 8.		Inspected the animals of 100th Inf. Brigade. Was admitted to hospital, suffering from severe contusion of left hip, caused by a kick, received from a horse. During Major Plunkett's absence, Captain Salor A.V.C. takes over the duties of A.D.V.S.	✓
"	" 9.		Individually examined all horses in No 3 Section D.A.C. for suspected skin lesions.	✓
"	" 10		Inspected the animals of No 3 Coy Train for symptoms of Contagious Stomatitis.	✓
"	" 11		Inspected animals of No 2 Coy Train and No 1 Section No. D.A.C. General condition of all animals satisfactory.	✓
"	" 12		Ordinary routine and office duties	✓
"	" 13		Inspected the animals of 33 Divisional Headquarters. Condition of all animals good. Shoeing up to date.	✓

Army Form C. 2118.

WAR DIARY of Captain O.G.E Salon
ADVS 33 Divn
INTELLIGENCE SUMMARY.
(Erase heading not required.)

Instructions regarding War Diaries and Intelligence Summaries are contained in F.S. Regs., Part II. and the Staff Manual respectively. Title pages will be prepared in manuscript.

Place	Date	Hour	Summary of Events and Information	Remarks and references to Appendices
LONG	JAN 14		Individual examination of all horses in No 3 Section D.A.C. for suspicious skin disease	
"	" 15		Accompanied D.D.V.S. Fourth Army on inspection of No 3 Section D.A.C.	
"	" 16		Accompanied Major Wadly on inspection of the animals in No 3 Section D.A.C.	
"	" 17		Individually examined all horses in No 3 Coy Train for symptoms of Contagious Stomatitis	
"	" 18		Moved from LONG to CHIPILLY.	
CHIPILLY	" 19		Ordinary routine and office duties.	
"	" 20		Inspected animals of 33 Signal Coy R.E.	
"	" 21		Visited the A.D.V.S and M.V.S 110th Division to arrange for the return of personnel, sent to 51st M.V.S.	
"	" 22		Visited new area and inspected horse lines for 45th M.V.S.	
"	" 23		Moved from CHIPILLY to SUZANNE. Office in the Chateau.	
"	" 24		Inspected new area with view to locating infected stables and camps	
"	" 25		Inspected animals of 19th Infantry Brigade. General condition of all animals good, and very well stabled.	

Army Form C. 2118.

WAR DIARY of Captain A.G.E Salor MC
or
INTELLIGENCE SUMMARY.

of 90 D.A.S, 33 Div.

(Erase heading not required.)

Instructions regarding War Diaries and Intelligence Summaries are contained in F. S. Regs., Part II. and the Staff Manual respectively. Title pages will be prepared in manuscript.

Place	Date	Hour	Summary of Events and Information	Remarks and references to Appendices
SUZANNE	Jan 26		Inspected 33 Divisional Train at Barogh 3 LANEUVILLE, also examined horses attached from 40th Division	
"	" 27		Ordinary routine and office duties.	
"	" 28		Visited the A.D.V.S 5th Division with regard to Glanders cases in N°1 Section D.A.C, and took over administration of that Unit and N°2 Section D.A.C.	
"	" 29		Inspected the animals of Sections 1 & 2 D.A.C. General condition of all animals good, and well started.	
"	" 30		Inspected the animals of 162 Brigade R.F.A. Condition satisfactory	
"	" 31		Attended conference of A.D's.V.S. at 4th Army Headquarters.	

In the Field.

B.J.T.ololo Goffan Alt.
X/o A.D.V.S, 33rd Divn.

WAR DIARY of Captain A.G. Roberts A/C
or
O/C. D.O.V.S. 33 Division

INTELLIGENCE SUMMARY.
(Erase heading not required.)

Army Form C. 2118.

Vol/6

Place	Date	Hour	Summary of Events and Information	Remarks and references to Appendices
SUZANNE	1917 Feb 1st		Inspected all animals at 143rd 97 F.A.S.	
"	" 2		Inspected Rear and Advanced Head quarter Horses. General condition good. Stabling satisfactory.	
"	" 3		Inspected No 1 & 2 Sections 33rd D.A.C. Horses of both Units are in good condition. Large number of "Bruised Soles" and "Thrush" caused by frozen ground. Box stoves are being adapted to prevent this, with good results.	
"	" 4		Inspected main watering point on BRAY-SUZANNE ROAD. Complained to Town Major SUZANNE re. the bad condition of standings at this watering point, owing to frost. He arranged to supply materials and labour to improve this standing.	
"	" 5		Inspected animals of 156 Brigade R.F.A. General condition of all animals satisfactory.	
"	" 6		Inspected all animals at "M.V.S."	
"	" 7		Inspected 101st Infantry Brigade R.F.O, 11th, 222nd Field Coy R.E. all the animals are in satisfactory condition, with exception of No 7 Coy R.E. where many animals are in a debilitated condition.	
"	" 8		Ordinary routine and office duties.	
"	" 9		Inspected animals at 143rd 97 M.S.	

Army Form C. 2118.

WAR DIARY of Captain. O. G. Chater. MC
o/c A.D.V.S. 33 Division
or
INTELLIGENCE SUMMARY.
(Erase heading not required.)

Instructions regarding War Diaries and Intelligence Summaries are contained in F. S. Regs., Part II. and the Staff Manual respectively. Title pages will be prepared in manuscript.

Place	Date	Hour	Summary of Events and Information	Remarks and references to Appendices
	1917			
SUZANNE	Feb 10		Inspected animals of 212th F. Cy. R.E. General condition good. Inspection of 18th Middlesex, condition satisfactory	
"	" 11		Inspected animals of 156 Brigade R.F.A. General condition of all animals satisfactory	
"	" 12		Inspected 100th M.G.C. Animals with this Unit are in good condition	
"	" 13		Inspected 162 Brigade R.F.A. General condition satisfactory	

O. G. Chater
Captain. MC

Army Form C. 2118.

WAR DIARY of Major T.O. Plunkett. AVC
or
N.O.D.O.S. 33 Division
INTELLIGENCE SUMMARY.
(Erase heading not required.)

Instructions regarding War Diaries and Intelligence Summaries are contained in F.S. Regs, Part II. and the Staff Manual respectively. Title pages will be prepared in manuscript.

Place	Date	Hour	Summary of Events and Information	Remarks and references to Appendices
SUZANNE	1917 Feb 14		Returned to duty. Attended conference of O.D.'s D.A.C. at 4th Army Headquarters.	N.A.P
"	" 15		Inspected animals of 9th Highland Light Infantry and selected six suffering from Debility for evacuation to 4th Gos on Pas.	N.A.P
"	" 16		Inspected No.1. Section D.A.C. Condition of all animals satisfactory.	N.A.P
"	" 17		Inspected Head Quarters 162 Brigade R.F.A. General condition satisfactory.	N.A.P
"	" 18		Inspected A.B & C Batteries 162 Brigade R.F.A. General condition of all animals satisfactory.	N.A.P
"	" 19		Inspected animals of 11th, 212th, 222nd Field Coy R.E. and 15th Middlesex Pioneers. General condition satisfactory, with exception of 11th F. Coy R.E., which are had (these animals are recently extra ration (Crushed Oats and Bran)	N.M.
"	" 20		Inspected No.2 Section D.A.C., 4th Kings Liverpool Regt, 2nd A & S.H. Battalion 98th Machine Gun Coy. The condition of animals in No.2 Section D.A.C. 10 satisfactory, with exception of sixteen animals which are receiving attention. 4th Kings in excellent condition. 98th M.G.C. satisfactory with exception of mules which ought to be improved. 2nd A & S.H. Battalion fair	N.A.P

Army Form C. 2118.

Instructions regarding War Diaries and Intelligence
Summaries are contained in F. S. Regs., Part II.
and the Staff Manual respectively. Title pages
will be prepared in manuscript.

WAR DIARY of Major K.O. Plunkett. AVC
No. 2. D.of.S. 33 Division

INTELLIGENCE SUMMARY.
(Erase heading not required.)

Place	Date	Hour	Summary of Events and Information	Remarks and references to Appendices
	1917			
SUZANNE	Feb 21		Inspected 1st Queens, 2nd Worcesters, 16 K.R.R., 19th R.F., 19th H.L.I. All animals are looking well with exception of register in 19th H.L.I. These animals are receiving extra ration (linseed cake and bran). Six of the animals from this battalion are under treatment in H 3rd M.V.S.	W.M?
"	22		Inspected 14th Brigade R.F.A. & D.A.C. (attached). General condition satisfactory with exception of a small number of "light draughts" in the D.A.C. which are in poor condition	W.M?
"	23		Inspected 1st Middlesex, 4th Suffolks. "D" Battery 162 Brigade R.F.A. Condition of animals good, with exception of "D"/162 Bde/R.F.A. which are unsatisfactory	W.M?
"	24		Inspected 33rd Signal Coy. R.E. 11th H Section 33rd D.A.C. "M.M.P." Condition of all animals good.	W.M?
"	25		Inspected animals of Advanced & Rear Headquarters horses. Condition good	W.M?
"	26		Inspected 19th Machine Gun Coy. Condition of animals fair. Reports to Brigade "A" and "D". 20th Royal Fusiliers, 2 L Royal Welsh Fusiliers. Condition satisfactory	W.M?
"	27		Inspected 5th Scottish Rifles. Marvel "Draughts" in light condition and are receiving special attention. 1st Hammersmiths in satisfactory condition. Inspected then horses of 2nd A.T.F. H. Btm, 1st Middlesex, 11th F. Cy. R.E. Marked improvement in condition	W.M?

Army Form C. 2118.

WAR DIARY of Major R.O. Plunkett. ADC
of ADVS, 33 Division

or

INTELLIGENCE SUMMARY.

(Erase heading not required.)

Instructions regarding War Diaries and Intelligence Summaries are contained in F. S. Regs., Part II. and the Staff Manual respectively. Title pages will be prepared in manuscript.

Place	Date	Hour	Summary of Events and Information	Remarks and references to Appendices
SUZANNE	1917 Feb 27		Inspected these animals since my previous inspection. Inspected 156 Brigade T.T.O. General condition of animals satisfactory	ADVS. M.D.
"	" 28			

R. Plunkett Major ADC
ADVS/33 Divn

Army Form C. 2118.

WAR DIARY of Major R.O. Plunkett, A.V.C.
A.D.V.S. 33rd Division
INTELLIGENCE SUMMARY.
(Erase heading not required.)

Instructions regarding War Diaries and Intelligence Summaries are contained in F.S. Regs., Part II. and the Staff Manual respectively. Title pages will be prepared in manuscript.

Place	Date	Hour	Summary of Events and Information	Remarks and references to Appendices
SUZANNE	Sept 1st		Attended conference of A.D.V.S. at Fourth Army	
"	" 2		Inspected sick animals of "D" Battery 162 Brigade R.F.A. Improving in condition.	
"	" 3		Inspected the animals of No. 1 and 2 sections D.A.C. Condition good.	
"	" 4		Ordinary routine and office duties	
"	" 5		Inspected animals of 1st & C. Middlesex Pioneers and S.T.C. Condition satisfactory.	
"	" 6		Inspected all animals under treatment in M.V.S.	
"	" 7		Inspection of 19th F. Ambulance. With exception of "3 Heavy Draughts" the condition of this Unit is satisfactory.	
"	" 8		Inspected new site for M.V.S. at CORBIE.	
"	" 9		Moved from SUZANNE to CORBIE.	
"	" 10		Inspected mules of 98th C. Machine Gun Coy. Condition poor. Inspected Remounts of 19th Infantry Brigade and 11th F. Coy R.E.	
"	" 11		Ordinary routine and office duties.	
CORBIE	" 12		Inspected following units :- 1st Middlesex, condition of all animals satisfactory. 11th F. Coy R.E. Condition improving. 9th H.L.I. Condition much improved. Inspected all sick animals for evacuation at M.V.S.	

Army Form C. 2118.

WAR DIARY of Major R.O. Blunfett, N.C.
or A.D.V.S. 33 Division
INTELLIGENCE SUMMARY.
(Erase heading not required.)

Instructions regarding War Diaries and Intelligence Summaries are contained in F. S. Regs., Part II. and the Staff Manual respectively. Title pages will be prepared in manuscript.

Place	Date	Hour	Summary of Events and Information	Remarks and references to Appendices
CORBIE	March 13		Inspected "D" battery 162 Bde. R.F.A. This Unit with exception of thirteen animals is much improved. Inspected Headquarters 162 Bde R.F.A. Condition very good.	W.
"	" 14		Inspected L.H.Q., C.R.A., M.M.P., D.H.Q. Condition of all animals excellent. Inspected 33rd Signal Coy R.E. Condition satisfactory. Grooming requires attention.	W.P.
"	" 15		Inspected "B" & "C" batteries 162 Bde R.F.A. Condition of all animals good.	W.P.
"	" 16		Inspected No. 1 & 2 Sections 33rd D.A.C. Condition of No. 1 Section most satisfactory. Condition of No. 2 Section satisfactory with exception of eleven animals which were evacuated suffering from Debility.	W.P.
"	" 17		Inspected following Units :- 5th Sentinel Coys. Condition of several "Draughts" unsatisfactory. 9 & 11 Machine Gun Coy. Condition of Mules het. 99% S. Condition of horses satisfactory.	W.P.
"	" 18		Inspected 1/5th Middlesex Pioneers. With exception of eight animals the condition of this Unit is satisfactory. Inspected all such animals for evacuation at H.3rd M.V.S.	W.P.
"	" 19		Attended Conference of A.D.V.S. at Fourth Army.	W.P.
"	" 20		Inspected 'B' Echelon D.A.C. Condition of all animals satisfactory.	W.P.

Army Form C. 2118.

WAR DIARY of Major R.O. Plunkett. MC
or A.D.V.S. 33 Division
INTELLIGENCE SUMMARY.
(Erase heading not required.)

Instructions regarding War Diaries and Intelligence Summaries are contained in F. S. Regs., Part II. and the Staff Manual respectively. Title pages will be prepared in manuscript.

Place	Date	Hour	Summary of Events and Information	Remarks and references to Appendices
CORBIE	March 21		Inspected the following units:- 1st Honourables. This Unit with exception of some draughts is in satisfactory condition. 2nd R.W. Fusiliers. Improving in condition. 19th Machine Gun Coy. Improvement in the condition of these animals. 9 FCo Machine Gun Coy. Condition satisfactory. The their animals of this Unit are receiving Chaff, Crushed corn and Bran.	N/A
"	" 22		Inspected 1st Middlesex and 1st Suffolks. Condition satisfactory. Inspected H.Q. Clattering 156 Bde R.F.A. Condition of "A" Battery good. Condition of "C" Battery satisfactory.	N/A
"	" 23		Inspected "B" + "D" Batteries 156 Bde R.F.A. Condition of "B" Battery fair. "D" Battery is in satisfactory condition.	N/A
"	" 24		Inspected 1/6 F. Coy R.E. These animals are receiving Bran and oats chaff ration daily.	N/A
"	" 25		Inspected 1/9 Infantry Brigade. General condition of all animals satisfactory.	N/A
"	" 26		Inspected the their animals of 5th Scottish Rifles and 1st Shamrockians. These animals show slight improvement. Inspected 19th F. Ambulance. Condition of animals good.	N/A
"	" 27		Inspected 33rd Signal Coy. R.E. General condition of animals satisfactory.	N/A

Army Form C. 2118.

WAR DIARY of Major R.O. Plunkett. AVC
of A.D.V.S. 33rd Div'n
INTELLIGENCE SUMMARY.
(Erase heading not required.)

Instructions regarding War Diaries and Intelligence Summaries are contained in F. S. Regs., Part II. and the Staff Manual respectively. Title pages will be prepared in manuscript.

Place	Date	Hour	Summary of Events and Information	Remarks and references to Appendices
CORBIE	March 28		Inspected 11th F. Coy. R.E. All the animals of this Unit owing to greater care are improving in condition. Grooming is receiving more attention	N.A.R.
"	" 29		Inspected 101st F. Ambulance. General condition excellent.	N.A.R.
"	" 30		Inspected 2nd A. & S. H. Bttn. Condition of animals satisfactory.	N.A.R.
"	" 31		Inspected 18th Middlesex Pioneers. Condition improved.	N.A.R.

2.4.17

N.A. Plunkett Major AVC
A.D.V.S. 33 Division

Army Form C. 2118.

WAR DIARY of Major R.O. Hewlett MC

INTELLIGENCE SUMMARY of A.D.V.S. 33rd Division

(Erase heading not required.)

Instructions regarding War Diaries and Intelligence Summaries are contained in F.S. Regs., Part II. and the Staff Manual respectively. Title pages will be prepared in manuscript.

Place	Date	Hour	Summary of Events and Information	Remarks and references to Appendices
In the Field	April 1st		Inspected all animals under treatment at M.V.S.	M.A.P.
"	" 2nd		Ordinary routine and office duties.	M.A.P.
"	" 3rd		Moved from COISIE to BEAUVAL. Inspected new site for M.V.S.	M.A.P.
"	" 4th		Inspected the animals and lines of 115 F. Coy. R.E.	M.A.P.
"	" 5th		Moved from BEAUVAL to LUCHEUX	M.A.P.
"	" 6th		Reported arrival in this area to D.D.V.S. Third Army	M.A.P.
"	" 7th		Moved from LUCHEUX to POMMIER	M.A.P.
"	" 8th		Inspected Horse Lines of 1st Queens and 19th Middlesex Officers.	M.A.P.
"	" 9th		Inspected the animals of 212th F. Coy. R.E.	M.A.P.
"	" 10th		Inspected the following Units :- 98th Machine Gun Coy. Condition of this Unit is much improved. 99th F. Ambulance, Condition good, 2nd Royal Welsh Fusiliers. This Unit is improving in condition, 19th Machine Gun Coy. Engineers in condition. "B" Echelon D.A.C. Inspected the their animals of this Unit and arranged for the removal of same to A.S.I M.V.S.	M.A.P.
"	" 11th		Ordinary routine and office duties.	M.A.P.
"	" 12th		Moved from POMMIER to BAIZIEVILLE	M.A.P.
"	" 13th		Inspected the animals and lines of 33rd Signal Coy. R.E.	M.A.P.

A.834 Wt. W.4973 M687 750,000 8/16 D.D. & L. Ltd. Forms/C.2118/13.

Army Form C. 2118.

WAR DIARY of Major R.A. Hunter DSO
or
INTELLIGENCE SUMMARY.
A.D.V.S. 33 Division

(Erase heading not required.)

Instructions regarding War Diaries and Intelligence Summaries are contained in F. S. Regs., Part II. and the Staff Manual respectively. Title pages will be prepared in manuscript.

Place	Date	Hour	Summary of Events and Information	Remarks and references to Appendices
In the Field	April 14th		Inspected animals of "B" Echelon D.A.C. Condition satisfactory. 2nd R.W. Fusiliers. Horses of this Unit have improved in condition. 19th Bn M.G. Coy. This Unit appears to have lost condition since my last inspection. A greater effort might be made to improve the grooming. 19th F.A. Ambulance, condition satisfactory.	M.A.O.
"	" 15th		Moved from BRAINEVILLE to HAMAINCOURT. Inspected the watering points in this area.	M.A.O.
"	" 16th		Inspected animals of No 2 Coy Train. Many horses in this Unit have lost condition. Inspected No 3-4 Coy Train. General condition satisfactory.	M.A.O.
"	" 17th		Inspected animals and horses of 9th A.S.C. Condition of animals moderate.	M.A.O.
"	" 18th		Inspected the animals of 124th Brigade R.F.O. (attached) Condition fair. Worst cases are being evacuated.	M.A.O.
"	" 19th		Inspected animals of "C" Battery 123rd Brigade R.F.O. Condition of this Battery is bad.	M.A.O.
"	" 20th		Inspected 18th Middlesex Pioneers. With exception of "2.I.D." the condition of this Unit is satisfactory.	M.A.O.
"	" 21st		Inspected the animals of 150th Army F.A. Brigade (attached). Condition of animals satisfactory.	M.A.O.
"	" 22nd		Inspected animals and horses of 11th F. Coy R.E.	M.A.O.

WAR DIARY of Major R.O. Plunkett MC
or
INTELLIGENCE SUMMARY. of A.D.V.S. 33 Division

Army Form C. 2118.

(Erase heading not required.)

Place	Date	Hour	Summary of Events and Information	Remarks and references to Appendices
In the Field	April 23rd		Ordinary routine and office duties	M.V.P.
"	" 24th		Inspected 120 animals for evacuation at 4-3rd M.V.S.	M.V.P.
"	" 25th		Inspected animals under treatment in M.V.S.	M.V.P.
"	" 26th		Moved from HAMELINCOURT to ADINFER.	1/M.
"	" 27th		Inspected animals of "D" Section 3rd Labour Coy R.E. Animals improving	M.V.P.
"	" 28th		Inspected 98th Infantry Brigade and 99th Field Ambulance. General condition satisfactory.	M.V.P.
"	" 29th		Inspected animals at 4-3rd M.V.S.	M.V.P.
"	" 30th		Inspected 19th Infantry Brigade. General condition satisfactory.	M.V.P.

R. Plunkett Major A.V.C.
A.D.V.S. 33 Division

Army Form C. 2118.

WAR DIARY of Major R.O. Clarkett MC
A.D.V.S. 33rd Division
or INTELLIGENCE SUMMARY.
(Erase heading not required.)

Vol 19

Instructions regarding War Diaries and Intelligence Summaries are contained in F. S. Regs., Part II. and the Staff Manual respectively. Title pages will be prepared in manuscript.

Place	Date	Hour	Summary of Events and Information	Remarks and references to Appendices
In the Field	1.5.17		Inspected the animals of 2nd Infantry Brigade. The then animals of 1/5th Scottish Rifles, 1st Queen's and 2nd Royal Welsh Fusiliers much improved. General condition of all animals satisfactory.	1/W.
"	2.5.17		Inspected animals under treatment in H.31st M.V.S.	1/W.
"	3.5.17		Inspected animals of 2nd Worcesters and "B" Echelon D.A.C. General condition satisfactory.	1/W.
"	4.5.17		Ordinary routine and office duties.	1/W.
"	5.5.17		Inspected the animals of 1/5th Scottish Rifles. General condition satisfactory. Making arrangements satisfactory. Adequate supply.	1/W.
"	6.5.17		Visited animals for evacuation at M.V.S.	1/W.
"	7.5.17		Inspected 19th Machine Gun Coy. Condition much improved. All the animals are keep good.	1/W.
"	8.5.17		Completed animals of 1/5 S.Coy. R.C. The animals of this unit are improving in condition.	1/W.
"	9.5.17		Inspected 1st Cameronians. The greater number of their horses are now looking well.	1/W.
"	10.5.17		Inspected animals of 2nd Worcesters and "B" Echelon D.A.C. Condition good.	1/W.
"	11.5.17		Selected men and for H.31st M.V.S. and inspected the watering arrangements for horses at Bonbres-en-ment.	1/W.
"	12.5.17		Move from ADINFER to HAMEAINCOURT. Watering, water and office duties.	1/W.

WAR DIARY of Major R.O. Plunkett, MC
or A.D.V.S. 33 Division
INTELLIGENCE SUMMARY.

(Erase heading not required.)

Army Form C. 2118.

Instructions regarding War Diaries and Intelligence Summaries are contained in F. S. Regs., Part II. and the Staff Manual respectively. Title pages will be prepared in manuscript.

Place	Date	Hour	Summary of Events and Information	Remarks and references to Appendices
In the field	13.5.17		Inspected animals of "B" Echelon D.A.C. Wounded by shell fire	M.P.
"	14.5.17		Inspected 181st Cavalry Coy R.E, and 132 A.T Coy R.E. (attached). Stable management good.	M.P.
"	15.5.17		Inspected 98th Infantry Brigade. Condition of 1/5th Middlesex moderate, 2nd D. & 1st Staff, testing well. Satisfactory. Also inspected 2nd and 4th King's Reinforcement Depot, looking well. Game of A.V.C. Sergeants attached 33rd Division for my inspection of Veterinary Wallets and field Veterinary Base Books. Veterinary equipment complete in all particulars.	M.P. M.P.
"	16.5.17		Orderly routine and office duties.	M.P.
"	17.5.17		Inspected the following Units:- 21st Royal Fusiliers, condition satisfactory. 2nd Royal Welsh Fusiliers much improved. 1st Kings, 16th K.R.R. horses exceptionally good. Watering arrangements of all units Satisfactory.	M.P.
"	18.5.17		Inspected No 16 Coy Train. Many of the horses in this Unit are losing their winter coats, but with the exception of 3 animals the condition is satisfactory.	M.P.
"	19.5.17		Inspected 293rd Army F.A. Brigade. With exception of "B" Battery, condition of animals is fair. "C" Battery has many thin horses. Inspected 3.55. A.T. Coy R.E. Condition satisfactory.	M.P.
"	20.5.17		Inspected animals under treatment in No 3rd M.V.S.	M.P.

WAR DIARY of Major W.A. Plunkett, N.C.
or
INTELLIGENCE SUMMARY. A.D.V.S. 33 Division

Army Form C. 2118.

(Erase heading not required.)

Instructions regarding War Diaries and Intelligence Summaries are contained in F.S. Regs., Part II. and the Staff Manual respectively. Title pages will be prepared in manuscript.

Place	Date	Hour	Summary of Events and Information	Remarks and references to Appendices
In the field	21.5.17		Ordinary routine and office duties.	W.R.
"	22.5.17		Visited waggon lines of 19th Middlesex Pioneers and ascertained as to the suitability of grazing for their animals. Strong grd. of an animals required, stressing on the obligation of owning care to the place.	W.R.
"	23.5.17		Visited 35th Machine Gun Coy. The animals of this unit are improving in condition.	W.R.
"	24.5.17		Inspected the animals of 1st Field Ambulance. Condition satisfactory.	W.R.
"	25.5.17		Inspected 222 C.M.C. Condition of animals satisfactory.	W.R.
"	26.5.17		Inspected animals for treatment and evacuation at No. 31 M.V.S.	W.R.
"	27.5.17		Ordinary routine and office duties.	W.R.
"	28.5.17		Inspected 2nd D.V.S.H. Bttn. General condition satisfactory.	W.R.
"	29.5.17		Made arrangements for the issue of Anti-gas Respirators for horses to Units.	W.R.
"	30.5.17		Captain Leather, N.C. (T.C.) reported for duty with 156 Brigade R.F.A. in relief of Captain	W.R.
"	31.5.17		Eady, N.C. in accordance with Rar Army A.O. A.6526.	W.R.
"	31.5.17		Arrived from HOMERINCOURT to ADINFER.	W.R.

W.A. Plunkett
Major, N.C.
A.D.V.S. 33 Div.

WAR DIARY of Major S.A. Plunkitt, M.C.
INTELLIGENCE SUMMARY. D.A.D.V.S.
33rd Division Vol 2

Army Form C. 2118.

Place	Date	Hour	Summary of Events and Information	Remarks and references to Appendices
In the Field	1.6.17		Inspected animals and horses of 19th Machine Gun Coy. General condition of animals satisfactory.	11 D.V.
"	2.6.17		Inspected animals of 11th Field Coy R.E. Condition of this Unit is much improved.	11 D.V.
"	3.6.17		Attended Conference of A.D.V.S. at Third Army Headquarters.	11 D.V.
"	4.6.17		Inspected animals of 1/5th Scottish Rifles and 20th Royal Fusiliers. Condition of all animals satisfactory.	11 D.V.
"	5.6.17		Inspected "B" Echelon 33rd D.A.C. General condition of animals satisfactory. Slight defects in shoeing pointed out to Officer present. Demonstration given to N.Co's 15 and over, of the correct method of adjusting the Anti-Gas Horse Respirator.	11 D.V.
"	6.6.17		Inspected 4th Kings Liverpool Regt, 2nd A.S.A. Bttn and 98th Machine Gun Coy. General condition of all animals satisfactory.	11 D.V.
"	7.6.17		Inspected all animals for evacuation at 43rd Mobile Veterinary Section.	11 D.V.
"	8.6.17		Inspected animals and horses of 9th A.S.A. and 100th Machine Gun Coy. General condition of all animals satisfactory.	11 D.V.
"	9.6.17		Inspected 1 & 2 Field Coy S.E. All animals in this unit are looking well. Slight	11 D.V.

Army Form C. 2118.

WAR DIARY of Major J.A. Plunkett, MC
INTELLIGENCE SUMMARY. D.A.D.V.S.
33 Division

(Erase heading not required.)

Instructions regarding War Diaries and Intelligence Summaries are contained in F.S. Regs., Part II. and the Staff Manual respectively. Title pages will be prepared in manuscript.

Place	Date	Hour	Summary of Events and Information	Remarks and references to Appendices
In the Field	10.6.17		Inspected animals and lines of 2nd Royal Welsh Fusiliers. General condition satisfactory.	NP
"	11.6.17		Ordinary routine and office duties.	NP
"	12.6.17		Inspected 150 Remounts on arrival at railhead. General condition satisfactory.	NP
"	13.6.17		Inspected 2nd Worcesters and 100th Infantry Brigade Headquarters. General condition of all animals satisfactory. Slight defects in shoeing pointed out to transport officers.	NP
"	14.6.17		Inspected 11th F. Coy R.E. and 18th Middlesex Pioneers. Shoeing of 18th Middlesex good. 11th F. Coy R.E. satisfactory.	NP
"	15.6.17		Inspected animals under treatment at 43rd Mobile Veterinary Section.	NP
"	16.6.17		Inspected 19th F. Ambulance and 4th Suffolks. Condition of animals good. Shoeing satisfactory.	NP
"	17.6.17		Ordinary routine and office duties.	NP
"	18.6.17		Inspected N.N. Horses. General condition satisfactory. Shoeing satisfactory.	NP
"	19.6.17		Visited Waggon lines of 1/2 Glamorganshires and inspected the shoeing of their units.	NP

WAR DIARY of Major R.O. Plunkett, MC
D.A.D.V.S.
INTELLIGENCE SUMMARY
33 Division

Army Form C. 2118.

(Erase heading not required.)

Place	Date	Hour	Summary of Events and Information	Remarks and references to Appendices
In the Field	9.6.17		Moved from ADINFER to HAMELINCOURT.	Map.
	21.6.17		Proceeded on 10 days leave to England. Capt. Kales, MC. +St Mobile Veterinary Section takes over duties of A.D.V.S. during my absence.	Map.

R.A. Plunkett Major. MC
D.A.D.V.S. 33 Divn

WAR DIARY of Major A.A. Plunkett, VC
or
INTELLIGENCE SUMMARY. D.A.D.V.S. 33 Division

Army Form C. 2118.

Vol 21

(Erase heading not required.)

Place	Date	Hour	Summary of Events and Information	Remarks and references to Appendices
In the Field	2.7.17		Returned to duty off 10 days leave of absence.	MVS
"	3.7.17		Moved from AZINFER WOOD to VIKKERS BOCAGE. Inspected new site for H.31. MVS	MVS
"	4.7.17		Inspected all animals at H.31. MVS.	MVS
"	5.7.17		Moved from VIKKERS-BOCAGE to CAVISSON. Inspected Horse lines of Divisional Headquarters.	MVS
"	6.7.17		Inspected new site of H.31. MVS, and visited Horse lines of Headquarters Divisional Train.	MVS
"	7.7.17		Inspected animals of 110th Machine Gun Coy. Condition of all animals satisfactory.	MVS
"	8.7.17		Ordinary routine and office duties.	MVS
"	9.7.17		Inspected 21st Royal Fusiliers, 5th Scottish Rifles, 2nd Royal Welch Fusiliers, 11th F. Coy. C.E. and 19th Machine Gun Coy. General condition of all animals satisfactory.	MVS
"	10.7.17		Inspected animals of 33rd Signal Co. R.E. Condition of this unit is very much improved.	MVS
"	11.7.17		Inspected animals of 1st Cameronians. A few h.D's in this unit are in slight condition. Attention of Transport Officer was called to a few horses that required shoeing.	MVS

WAR DIARY of Major G. A. Plunkett, MC
D.A.D.V.S. 33 Division

Army Form C. 2118.

INTELLIGENCE SUMMARY.
(Erase heading not required.)

Instructions regarding War Diaries and Intelligence Summaries are contained in F. S. Regs., Part II. and the Staff Manual respectively. Title pages will be prepared in manuscript.

Place	Date	Hour	Summary of Events and Information	Remarks and references to Appendices
In the Field	12.9.17		Inspected animals for evacuation at 4 3rd M.V.S.	MP
-	13.9.17		Inspected Headquarters 98th Infantry Brigade Headquarters, 4th Kings, 4th Suffolks, 212th I Coy R.E. General condition satisfactory. Slight effects (in shoeing of 4th King) pointed out to Transport officer. Shoeing on the whole satisfactory.	MP
-	14.9.17		Ordinary routine and office duties	MP
-	15.9.17		Inspected animals under treatment at 4 3rd M.V.S.	MP
-	16.9.17		Inspected 1st Middlesex Regt all horses of this unit are looking well. Inspected animals of 2nd O.T.S.H. Btn General condition satisfactory.	MP
-	17.9.17		Ordinary routine and office duties.	MP
-	18.9.17		Ordinary routine and office duties.	MP
-	19.9.17		Inspected 100th Machine Gun Coy, 18th Middlesex Pioneers and 222 F Coy R.E. General condition of the animals good. Shoeing satisfactory.	MP
-	20.9.17		Inspected animals under treatment at 4th M.V.S.	MP
-	21.9.17		Inspected 100th Inf Brigade Headquarters, 1st Queens, 2nd Worcesters 9th A.S.L. Condition of animals satisfactory. Shoeing on the whole satisfactory.	MP

WAR DIARY of Major C.A. Plunkett MC
INTELLIGENCE SUMMARY. D.A.D.M.S. 33 Division

Army Form C. 2118.

(Erase heading not required.)

Place	Date	Hour	Summary of Events and Information	Remarks and references to Appendices
By Field	22.7.17		Ordinary routine and office duties.	Nil
-	23.7.17		Inspected 215th Machine Gun Coy. Condition of animals satisfactory.	Nil
-	24.7.17		Inspected 16th King's Royal Rifles. Animals of this Unit are looking well. One Mange case removed from unit. Contacts dressed and segregated.	Nil
-	25.7.17		Inspected 98th Machine Gun Coy and 12th Middlesex Regt. All animals looking well.	Nil
-	26.7.17		Inspected Horse lines of 16th King's Royal Rifles.	Nil
-	27.7.17		Inspected No 2 & 4 Coys Train. Condition and stowing satisfactory. Inspected 2nd A. G.H. Btn. Condition and stowing satisfactory. Removed three cases of skin disease to 4.3rd M.V.S. for treatment.	Nil
-	28.7.17		Inspected No 3 Coy Train. Condition satisfactory. Animals free from skin disease.	Nil
-	29.7.17		Inspected animals of Divisional Head-quarters. Condition satisfactory.	Nil
-	30.7.17		Ordinary routine and office duties.	Nil
-	31.7.17		Moved from CAVIKOM to LA PANNE	Nil

C.A. Plunkett
D.A.D.V.S. 33 Div

WAR DIARY / INTELLIGENCE SUMMARY

Army Form C. 2118.

Major R.O. Blake A.V.C. D.O.D.V.S. 33 Division

Place	Date	Hour	Summary of Events and Information	Remarks and references to Appendices
In the Field	1.8.17		Visited horse lines of 143rd M.I.C. and inspected animals for evacuation.	
"	2.8.17		Inspected 14.5 Veterinary Sec. R.E. General condition of animals satisfactory, shoeing fair.	
"	3.8.17		Inspected 248 Machine Gun Coy. horses and shoeing of animals satisfactory.	M.D.S.
"	4.8.17		Attended Conference of D.A.D.V.S. at Tilques.	
"	5.8.17		Inspected animals of 99th F. Ambulance. General condition and shoeing satisfactory.	
"	6.8.17		Inspected 2nd & L.T. Btn. and 212 S.T. Coy. L.C. The animals of these units are in satisfactory condition.	
"	7.8.17		Inspected "B" Echelon 33rd D.A.C. Animals of this unit are looking well. The station of the Smallest Officer was called to a few animals which required shoeing.	W.M.D.
"	8.8.17		Inspected No.1 and 2 Sections 33rd D.A.C. Condition of No.1 section is satisfactory. A number of animals in No.2 Section D.A.C. are in half condition.	W.M.D.
"	9.8.17		Inspected animals of 19th Middlesex Pioneers. All animals of this unit are lively, well.	W.M.D.
"	10.8.17		Ordinary routine and office duties. Visited lines of 432 M.I.C. Inspected 100th Fd. Brigade. The animals of the "C" & "D" Coy. appear to have recently lost condition. Visited lines of 24th M.G. Coy. and inspected recently mobilised mules.	W.M.D.
"	11.8.17			W.M.D.

WAR DIARY of Major C.O. Thukes(?) MC

Army Form C. 2118.

INTELLIGENCE SUMMARY. D.O.D.V.S. 33 Division

Instructions regarding War Diaries and Intelligence Summaries are contained in F. S. Regs., Part II. and the Staff Manual respectively. Title pages will be prepared in manuscript.

(Erase heading not required.)

Place	Date	Hour	Summary of Events and Information	Remarks and references to Appendices
In the Field	12.8.17		Attended conference of D.O.D.V.S. at Thekla.	M.N.P.
			Inspected animals wounded by shell fire on "B" Lechila D.A.C., also inspected animals of A1 Gro Cy Frans. Animals of this unit are looking well. Arrangements being made for a better water supply for this unit.	
-	13.8.17		Inspected 4 & 5 Labour Coy's C.E. General condition of animals as satisfactory.	M.N.P.
-	14.8.17		Inspected 156 Brigade R.F.A. Animals of this Brigade are looking well, with the exception of a few in "D" Battery.	M.N.P.
-	15.8.17		Inspected horses for evacuation at 1/3rd M.V.S.	
-	16.8.17		Visited lines of 156 Brigade, 162 Brigade, H.Q. Suffolks, and 1st Wiltshires Inft., and inspected the horses in these units considered unfit for hard work as an aid to demobilisation.	M.N.P.
-	17.8.17		Visited horse lines of 1/21 + 2 Victoria D.A.C. and selected such horses as considered fit for hard work as an aid to demobilisation.	M.N.P.
-	18.8.17		Rode from LA PANNE to COXYDE BAINS. Inspected animal routes and offices this date. Attended conference of D.O.D.V.S. + 15th Corps Headquarters.	M.N.P.
-	19.8.17		Inspected animals awaiting evacuation at 1/3 M.V.S.	M.N.P.

WAR DIARY of Major J.O. Plunkett MC
or
INTELLIGENCE SUMMARY. D.A.D.V.S. 33 Division

Army Form C. 2118.

Place	Date	Hour	Summary of Events and Information	Remarks and references to Appendices
In the field	20.8.17		Inspected 212.A I Coy T.C. General condition of the unit is satisfactory.	
-	21.8.17		Inspected animals of 156 Mobile Vet. Section. General condition satisfactory.	M.V.S.
-	22.8.17		Inspected Div. H. Qrs., 33 Signal Coy., A.T. Mobile Section and B.T. Mobile Section. All the animals of these units are looking well.	
-	23.8.17		Inspected animals under treatment at 33 M.V.S.	M.V.S.
-	24.8.17		Games and inspection of horses considered fit for front line on dismobilization. Met the Remount Officer concerning watering arrangements.	
-	25.8.17		Inspected 222nd I Coy T.C. Condition of animals satisfactory. Watering arrangements satisfactory.	M.V.S.
-	26.8.17		Ordinary routine and office duties.	
-	27.8.17		Inspected "A" + "B" Batteries 156 Brigade, R.F.A. Condition and spring of "A" battery is good. Condition of "B" battery is good with the exception of 5 sick section which shows grey skin sores.	M.V.O.
-	28.8.17		Inspected "C" + "D" Batteries 156 Brigade R.F.A. Condition of animals and shoeing satisfactory.	M.V.O.
-	29.8.17		Inspected B.T. + A.T. Mobile Sections. Condition of animals satisfactory. Office moved from COXYDE BAINS to LA PANNE.	

WAR DIARY of Major E.O. Thickett RAC
or
INTELLIGENCE SUMMARY. D.A.D.M.S. 33 Division

Army Form C. 2118.

(Erase heading not required.)

Instructions regarding War Diaries and Intelligence Summaries are contained in F. S. Regs., Part II. and the Staff Manual respectively. Title pages will be prepared in manuscript.

Place	Date	Hour	Summary of Events and Information	Remarks and references to Appendices
In the field	31.8.19		Inspected "B" Echelon 33rd D.A.C. Condition of animals satisfactory.	Appx.
"	31.8.19		Ordinary routine and office duties.	A.W.

W.W. Thickett, Major RAC
D.A.D.M.S. 33 Division

WAR DIARY of Major C.A. Plunkett, VC
INTELLIGENCE SUMMARY. D.A.D.V.S. 33rd Division

Army Form C. 2118.

Vol 23

Place	Date	Hour	Summary of Events and Information	Remarks and references to Appendices
In the field	1.9.17		Moved from les Prures to Eperlecques. Ordinary routine and office duties.	N.P.
"	2.9.17		Inspected animals and watering arrangements at 4 & 3rd M.V.S.	N.P.
"	3.9.17		Inspected animals of 19th M.G. Coy. Condition of this unit is satisfactory. Shoeing not receiving fair share of transmitted position of HD & L.D. Moderate, others fair attention of the Transport Officer called to the condition and shoeing. Inspected 20th Royal Fusiliers, 5th Lothian Rifles, 2nd Irish Fusiliers. General condition of all animals good, shoeing satisfactory. Inspected animals of 19th & 99th F. Ambulances. Condition of former satisfactory, shoeing of latter very good. Shoeing of latter needs attention. Condition of Officers present satisfactory.	N.P.
"	4.9.17			
"	5.9.17		Inspected of 9th Inf. Brigade Mondelim. 1st Middlesex moderate, 2nd R. & S.H. 3ten fair, 4th Kings looking well, 14th Suffolks in good condition, also M.G. Coy. Vet., shoeing needs attention. Trl. Bde 9 Fd. Amb. Bgde draught horses need attention, majority of others absent off parade. Ordinary routine and office duties	N.P.
"	6.9.17			N.P.

WAR DIARY of Maj. C.O. Ockett. AVC
or
INTELLIGENCE SUMMARY. D.A.D.V.S. 33 Division

Army Form C. 2118.

Place	Date	Hour	Summary of Events and Information	Remarks and references to Appendices
In the Field	7.9.17		Inspected animals under treatment at 43rd M.V.S.	
"	8.9.17		Visited horse lines of D.A.D. and arranged for a better water supply for animals.	
"	9.9.17		Took over command of 43rd M.V.S. during Captain Eaton's absence on leave.	1.V.S
"	10.9.17		Inspected animals of 19th Infantry Brigade. Condition and ordinary grooming and shoeing satisfactory.	
"	11.9.17		Inspected animals of A.V.Coles. Condition satisfactory. Shoeing up to date.	
"	12.9.17		Duties at 43rd M.V.S.	
"	13.9.17		Inspected remounts on arrival. Condition in L.D. + H.D. fair.	
"	14.9.17		Inspected animals of 11th Leicestershires. Condition and shoeing fair.	
"	15.9.17		Inspected animals. See wounters at 43rd M.V.S.	11.V.O
"	16.9.17		Move from EPERLECQUES to WESTIN--SE. Ordinary routine and office duties.	
"	17.9.17		Visited Wagon Lines of Div. Arty. Inspected new site for 43rd M.V.S.	
"	18.9.17		Visited M.V.S. and arranged for a better water supply for D.A.D., to improve to Y.O.S.	
"	19.9.17		Inspected 33rd Signal Cy. C.E. Condition of this unit is fair. Shoeing and grooming need attention.	111 -

WAR DIARY of Maj. E.O. Hunter MC
D.A.D.V.S. 33 Div
INTELLIGENCE SUMMARY

Army Form C. 2118.

(Erase heading not required.)

Instructions regarding War Diaries and Intelligence Summaries are contained in F.S. Regs., Part II. and the Staff Manual respectively. Title pages will be prepared in manuscript.

Place	Date	Hour	Summary of Events and Information	Remarks and references to Appendices
In the Field	20.9.17		Inspected No 1 Section 33rd D.A.C. Condition of mules good, horses moderate, shoeing moderate	
"	21.9.17		Inspected No 2 Section D.A.C. Grooming and general condition good. Shoeing of mules moderate, horses good.	
"	22.9.17		Attended conference of D.A.D.V.S. at I Corps Headquarters. Ordinary routine and office duties.	
"	23.9.17		Inspected pack mules at D.A.C. Mobile lines of 33 D.S.C.	
"	24.9.17		Ordinary routine and office duties.	
"	25.9.17		Moved from WESTOUTRE to LA-CLYTTE. Artillery regrouped. Division	
"	26.9.17		Inspected horse lines and watering arrangements in DICKEBUSCH area.	
"	27.9.17		Inspected 19th L. Brigade, 209 M.G. Coy, 2nd S.M.G. Coy. Animals in good condition, grooming and shoeing fair.	
"	28.9.17		Moved from LA CLYTTE to BARINGHEM. E.O. temporarily attached	
"	29.9.17		Ordinary routine and office duties.	
"	30.9.17		Ordinary routine and office duties.	

M.R. Hewlett Major
D.A.D.V.S. 33 Division

WAR DIARY of Major C.O. Platt? MC
D.A.D.V.S. 33 Division
INTELLIGENCE SUMMARY
Army Form C. 2118

Vol 24

Place	Date	Hour	Summary of Events and Information	Remarks and references to Appendices
In Field	1.10.17		Ordinary routine and office duties. Arrived with D.A.D.V.S. 5th Division for administration of A. Visits. L.C.B. and 1st Williams Pioneer Blot detailed in 10th Corps area.	
"	2.10.17		Visited A & B batteries 162 Brigade R.F.A. Horses fair.	
"	3.10.17		Ordinary routine and office duties.	
"	4.10.17		Inspected animals of D.H.Q. and A.V. Vet. Condition and shoeing good.	
"	5.10.17		Move from BRAINGHEM to WIZERNES.	
"	6.10.17		Move from WIZERNES to BOLLEZEELE. 432 M.S. to BOLLINGHEM area.	
"	7.10.17		Inspected mule gift for 432 M.S. who watering arrangements for D.H.Q. horses.	
"	8.10.17		Inspected animals at 432 M.S. also horse lines of 332 Signal Co. R.E.	
"	9.10.17		Move from BOLLEZEELE to B.H.Q. hospital. Inspected stables and watering arrangements for O.H.Q. horses.	
"	10.10.17		Inspected animals of 'B' Echelon D.A.C. General condition good.	
"	11.10.17		Inspected Box clipping shed and arranged with B. to proceed to commence clipping on the morning of 12th 10th inst.	
"	12.10.17		Visited 11th I.Co. L.C. and 1st Williams. General condition of all animals patisfactory.	
"	13.10.17		Attended conference of D.A.D.V.S. at VIII Corps Headquarters. Visited lines of 1.2.D.V.S.	

WAR DIARY or INTELLIGENCE SUMMARY

Army Form C. 2118.

Major C.A. Statt MC
D.A.D.V.S.
33 Division

Place	Date	Hour	Summary of Events and Information	Remarks and references to Appendices
In the Field	14.10.17		Ordinary routine and office duties	
"	15.10.17		Visited Dist stabling shed and superintended the clipping of horses	
"	16.10.17		Inspected sick lines 33 D.A.C. and horses also visited Dist clipping shed	
"	17.10.17		Superintended the clipping of horses at Dist clipping shed	
"	18.10.17		Visited horse lines of 99th F. Ambulance. Routine and office duties	
"	19.10.17		Ordinary routine and office duties	
"	20.10.17		Attended conference of D.A.D.V.S. at VIII Corps Headquarters	
"	21.10.17		Inspected the clipping of horses at Dist clipping shed. Routine and office duties	
"	22.10.17		Inspected horse lines of 18th Middlesex Division	
"	23.10.17		Visited Dist clipping shed. Routine and office duties	
"	24.10.17		Ordinary routine and office duties	
"	25.10.17		Granted 10 days leave to Ireland. Left Sta HQ etc to 3d M/G. Duties over taken by D.A.D.V.S. during my absence	
"	26.10.17		Routine and office duties	
"	27.10.17		Attended conference of D.A.D.V.S. at VIII Corps Headquarters	
"	28.10.17		Routine and office duties	

WAR DIARY / Adt A.D.C Sah. MC
INTELLIGENCE SUMMARY. 1/D A.D.M.S 33 Div

Army Form C. 2118.

Place	Date	Hour	Summary of Events and Information	Remarks and references to Appendices
In field	29.10.19		Inspected animals of 100th Infantry Brigade. Centers and office duties	
"	30.10.19		Reconnoised A.D.S. VIII Corps on inspection of suspicious case of doubtful Lymphangitis in 21st Battery 11th Brigade 3rd Australian Division.	
"	31.10.19		Centers and office duties.	

Callaro MC
for D.A.D.V.S
33 Division

WAR DIARY of Lattain O.L.L.Corps
or
INTELLIGENCE SUMMARY. 1 D.A.D15
(Erase heading not required.)

Army Form C. 2118.

Vol 25

Place	Date	Hour	Summary of Events and Information	Remarks and references to Appendices
G.H.Q.1st	1.11.19		Proceeded with A.D.V.S. 1st Corps to inspect animals of 41st Brigade R.F.A.	
"	2.11.19		Supervised the clipping of horses at the Divisional clothing station	
"	3.11.19		Attended conference of A.A.D.V.S. at A.D.V.S. Office 1st Corps	
"	4.11.19		Ordinary routine and office duties	
"	5.11.19		Supervised the clipping of horses at the Divisional clothing station	
"	6.11.19		Inspected animals of 332 D.A.C. Routine and office duties	
"	7.11.19		Proceeded to C+D P.Sn area to inspect suspicious dermatitis case in 156 Brigade R.F.A.	
"	8.11.19		Attended Divisional clothing shed. Routine and office duties	
"	9.11.19		Supervised the clipping of horses at Div clothing station	
"	10&11.19		Attended conference of A.A.D.V.S. at 1st Corps Headquarters	
"	11.11.19		Ordinary routine and office duties	
"	12.11.19		332 Div clothing shed closed down for clipping of the Division horses, and is handed over to	
"	13.11.19		115th Div artillery with a nucleus of clipping machines and hand rings	
"	14.11.19		Ordinary routine and office duties	
"	15.11.19		Inspected animals of 1st Lt Bn Machine Gun Co	
"	16.11.19		Routine and office duties	

WAR DIARY 1/1yr COOLIES HC
or
INTELLIGENCE SUMMARY. D.A.D.V.S. 33rd Division.

(Erase heading not required.)

Army Form C. 2118.

Instructions regarding War Diaries and Intelligence Summaries are contained in F. S. Regs., Part II. and the Staff Manual respectively. Title pages will be prepared in manuscript.

Place	Date	Hour	Summary of Events and Information	Remarks and references to Appendices
In the Field	16.11.17		Our S.O. United W.C. returned from leave and resumed the duties of D.A.D.V.S.	
"	17.11.17		Proceeded to YPRES area to inspect new site for M.V.S. Inspected horse lines of D.A.C.	
"	18.11.17		Officer arrived from 6th Mounted Bde to 28th Bde DIV. H.Q. Cattle and other duties.	
"	19.11.17		Visited A.D.V.S. 58th Corps Head-quarters. Inspected animals at 142nd Mobile Vet. Section.	
"	20.11.17		Inspected animals of 100th Infantry Brigade. General condition of all animals most satisfactory.	
"	21.11.17		Inspected animals of 19th Infantry Brigade. General condition satisfactory. Inspected gun teams of 1st & 3rd M.V.S.	
"	22.11.17		Inspected watering arrangements for horse in BRANDHOEK area.	
"	23.11.17		Inspected 11th F. Coy. R.E. In condition of animals satisfactory.	
"	24.11.17		Attended conference of D.A.D.V.S. at 1st Corps Head-quarters.	
"	25.11.17		Visited lines of 1.3.C.O. Mobile Vet. Section.	
"	26.11.17		Proceeded to War Office LONDON to report for duty in INDIA. Subsequently Lieut. Col. A 105 H. 25.11.17. Lieut. D.Y.S. Lieut. W.C. Q.G. M.B. M.S. takes over temporary duties of D.A.D.V.S.	

WAR DIARY / Captain O.C. to Lieut. Mc / **Army Form C. 2118.**
or
INTELLIGENCE SUMMARY. / D.A.D.V.S. 33 Division
(Erase heading not required.)

Place	Date	Hour	Summary of Events and Information	Remarks and references to Appendices
In the Field	27.11.17		Ordinary routine and office duties	
"	28.11.17		Inspected the advanced Veterinary Aid Post. Routine and office duties	
"	29.11.17		Inspected animals of 12 Hussars and 19 Machine Gun Cy. General condition satisfactory	
"	30.11.17		Routine and office duties	

Capt. D.A.D.V.S
4.12.17

[signature]
Captain Mc
A.D.V.S. 33 Division

WAR DIARY of Major G. H. Farrell MC
INTELLIGENCE SUMMARY. D.A.D.V.S. 33 Division

Army Form C. 2118.

Place	Date	Hour	Summary of Events and Information	Remarks and references to Appendices
In the Field	4.12.19		Maj. G. H. Farrell MC assumes duties of D.A.D.V.S. 33rd Division vice Major R.A. Plunkett MC to ENGLAND 26.11.19	
"	5.12.19		Reported in person to the A.D.V.S. 16 Corps. Routine and office duties	
"	6.12.19		Inspected horses and stabling of 33rd D.A.C. Condition of horses 90% Routine and office duties	
"	7.12.19		Inspected horses and stabling of No 32nd Mobile Veterinary Section. Presided over conference of Veterinary Officers attached 33 Division. Routine and office duties	
"	8.12.19		Attended conference of D.A.D.V.S. at 16 Corps Headquarters. Inspected animals of No 2-3 and 4 Corps Rein Train. Routine and office duties	
"	9.12.19		Routine and office duties	
"	10.12.19		Inspected animals of 33rd Division P.I.O. and D.A.C. Routine and office duties	
"	11.12.19		Inspected animals at No 32nd Mobile Veterinary Section	
"	12.12.19		Routine and office duties	
"	13.12.19		Office moved from BRANDHOEK to STEENVOORDE. Visited stables of 33rd D.A.C.	
"	14.12.19		Inspected animals of 33rd Wagon Coy etc. Daily routine and office duties	
"	15.12.19		Attended conference of D.A.D.V.S. at 16 Corps Headquarters. Routine and office duties	
"	16.12.19		Inspected animals and standings of No 2 M.V.S. Routine and office duties	

Army Form C. 2118.

WAR DIARY / Major J. H. Farrell N.C.
of D.A.D.V.S. 33 Division
INTELLIGENCE SUMMARY.

(Erase heading not required.)

Instructions regarding War Diaries and Intelligence Summaries are contained in F. S. Regs., Part II. and the Staff Manual respectively. Title pages will be prepared in manuscript.

Place	Date	Hour	Summary of Events and Information	Remarks and references to Appendices
In the Field	17.12.17		Inspected animals of 98th Infantry Brigade. Routine and office duties.	
"	18.12.17		Inspected animals and standings of 33 D.H.Q., M.M.P., 33d Signal Coy R.E. and 98th Trench Mortar Battery.	
"	19.12.17		Gun Coy. Routine and office duties.	
"			Inspected animals and standings of 2nd & 5th Machine Gun Coy. Routine and office duties	
"	20.12.17		Inspected animals and standings of 1st Army Field Artillery Brigade. Routine and office duties.	
"	21.12.17		Daily routine and office duties.	
"	22.12.17		Attended conference of D.A.D.V.S. at St John's Headquarters. Routine and office duties	
"	23.12.17		Inspected animals of 33d Div. H. Qrs.	
"	24.12.17		Routine and office duties	
"	25.12.17		Daily routine & office duties	
"	26.12.17		Inspected animals of 33d Signal Coy R.E. Routine and office duties	
"	27.12.17		Daily routine and office duties	
"	28.12.17		Daily routine and office duties	
"	29.12.17		Attended conference of D.A.D.V.S. at St John Headquarters. Routine and office duties.	
"	30.12.17		Daily routine and office duties.	

WAR DIARY of Major J. H. Farrell MC D.A.D.V.S. 33 Division
INTELLIGENCE SUMMARY

Army Form C. 2118.

(Erase heading not required.)

Instructions regarding War Diaries and Intelligence Summaries are contained in F. S. Regs., Part II. and the Staff Manual respectively. Title pages will be prepared in manuscript.

Place	Date	Hour	Summary of Events and Information	Remarks and references to Appendices
In the Field	3/1/15		Inspected 33rd Signal Coy's Stables and office later	JHF

J.H.Farrell Major VS
D.A.D.V.S. 33 Division

WAR DIARY
or
INTELLIGENCE SUMMARY.

(Erase heading not required.)

Army Form C. 2118.

N°4 D.A.D.V.S. 33 Division

Vol 27

Place	Date	Hour	Summary of Events and Information	Remarks and references to Appendices
In field	1.1.18		Visited stables of 33rd Div Headquarters. Routine and office duties	EGH
"	2.1.18		Inspected animals of 33 Divl Dilution Coy 9 Wilts. Routine and office duties	EGH
"	3.1.18		Inspected 33rd Signal Coy R.E. Colliery routine	EGH
"	4.1.18		Routine and office duties	EGH
"	5.1.18		Attended Inspection of D.A.D.V.S. at 1st Corps Headquarters	EGH
"	6.1.18		Went from STEENVOORDE to BANDHOEK. Routine and office duties	EGH
"	7.1.18		Inspected animals and standing at 437? with Veterinary Section	EGH
"	8.1.18		Inspected 33rd Divl Headquarters R.A. Routine and office duties	EGH
"	9.1.18		Inspected 33 Divl Headquarters and 91st Brigade Headquarters. Routine and office duties	EGH
"	10.1.18		Issued remounts to units of 33 Division. Prophets signed home left at F.E.C.R. 4	EGH
"	11.1.18		N° 2 Coy Labour. Routine and office duties	EGH
"	12.1.18		Presided over conference of D.A.D.V.S. 33 Division. Routine and office duties	EGH
"	13.1.18		Attended conference of D.A.D.V.S. at 1st Corps Headquarters. Routine and office duties	EGH
"	31.1.18		Granted 14 days leave to ENGLAND. Lt A.J.E. Cole V.C. etc A.D.V.S. took over duties of D.A.D.V.S. during my absence	EGH

Army Form C. 2118.

WAR DIARY
or
INTELLIGENCE SUMMARY.

1 Lt. R.A.A.C. Later H.C.
4/D.A.D.V.S. 33 Division

(Erase heading not required.)

Instructions regarding War Diaries and Intelligence Summaries are contained in F. S. Regs., Part II. and the Staff Manual respectively. Title pages will be prepared in manuscript.

Place	Date	Hour	Summary of Events and Information	Remarks and references to Appendices
In the Field	14.1.18		Visited horse lines of 33rd Div. Headquarters. Latrine and office duties	
"	15.1.18		Inspected animals of 33rd Divnl C.R.E.	
"	16.1.18		Latrine and office duties	
"	17.1.18		Inspected animals suffering from [mange] in 16 & 2 Brigade R.F.A. Latrine and office duties	
"	18.1.18		Latrine and office duties	
"	19.1.18		Attended conference of D.A.D.V.S. of XV Corps. Tent quarters Latrine and office duties	
"	20.1.18		Inspected animals of 19th Infantry Brigade	
"	21.1.18		Latrine and office duties	
"	22.1.18		Visited horse lines of 33 D.A.C. Office duties	
"	23.1.18		Inspected farm carts in 151 Brigade R.F.A.	
"	24.1.18		Latrine and office duties	
"	25.1.18		Visited lines of 33 Signal Coy. R.E. Office duties	
"	26.1.18		Attended conference of D.A.D.V.S. at 1st Echelon Headquarters	
"	27.1.18		Latrine and office duties	
"	28.1.18		Reported to Lieut. Col. [ ] H.C. relieve me [ ] 2nd Echelon lines of D.A.D.V.S. Division	

Army Form C. 2118.

WAR DIARY of No. 6 H Farrell H.C
or
INTELLIGENCE SUMMARY. D.A.D.V.S. 33 Division
(Erase heading not required.)

Place	Date	Hour	Summary of Events and Information	Remarks and references to Appendices
In the Field	29.7.18		Ordinary routine and office duties	
"	30.7.18		Good from BRANDHOEK to WIZERNES	
"	31.7.18		Inspected animals of 33rd Divn Headquarters division	

N. Farrell Capt HC
D.A.D.V.S. 33 Division

WAR DIARY or INTELLIGENCE SUMMARY.

Army Form C. 2118.

WAR DIARY of Major J. A. Farrell MC
D.A.D.V.S. 33 Division

Vol 28

Place	Date	Hour	Summary of Events and Information	Remarks and references to Appendices
In the Field	1.2.18		Inspected animals of Divisional Headquarters. Routine and office duties	JAF
"	2.2.18		Inspected animals and horse of O. i/c Cy 33 Div Train. Routine and office duties	JAF
"	3.2.18		Ordinary routine and office duties	JAF
"	4.2.18		Inspected all animals of Divisional Headquarters, on parade. Routine and office duties	JAF
"	5.2.18		Inspected equipment of personnel parading with A.D.V.S.	JAF
"	6.2.18		Inspected animals and horses of 33 Signal Co. RE. Routine and office duties	JAF
"	7.2.18		Routine and office duties	JAF
"	8.2.18		Routine and office duties	JAF
"	9.2.18		Routine and office duties	JAF
"	10.2.18		Routine and office duties	JAF
"	11.2.18		Routine and office duties	JAF
"	12.2.18		Routine and office duties	JAF
"	13.2.18		Routine and office duties	JAF
"	14.2.18		Routine and office duties	JAF
"	15.2.18		Routine and office duties	JAF
"	16.2.18		Routine and office duties	JAF

WAR DIARY or INTELLIGENCE SUMMARY.

Army Form C. 2118.

Major G. H. Farnell, A.V.C. D.A.D.V.S. 33 Division

(Erase heading not required.)

Instructions regarding War Diaries and Intelligence Summaries are contained in F. S. Regs., Part II. and the Staff Manual respectively. Title pages will be prepared in manuscript.

Place	Date	Hour	Summary of Events and Information	Remarks and references to Appendices
In the Field	17.2.18		Routine and office duties.	
-	18.2.18		Inspected animals at 33 Divisional Headquarters and 33 Signal Coy. R.E. Routine and office duties	
-	19.2.18		Inspected animals at No. 1 Coy Train and "B" Battery 162 Brigade R.F.A.	
-	20.2.18		Inspected animals and lines of 33 D.V.S. Routine and office duties	
-	21.2.18		Ordinary routine and office duties	
-	22.2.18		Ordinary routine and office duties	
-	23.2.18		Sent from VS 12 & 13 DVS to H.M.V.C.T.S. (Shut 2.B) Routine and office duties	
-	24.2.18		Inspected 33 DVS and 33 Div Train, "B" Battery 162 Brigade and 156 Bde R.F.A.	
-	25.2.18		Inspected 162 Brigade R.F.A., No. 1 Coy Train and 33 Signal Coy R.E.	
-	26.2.18		Inspected animals awaiting evacuation at 43 D.V.S. and No. 1 Coy 33 Div Train. Routine and office duties.	
-	27.2.18		Inspected animals at 43 D.V.S. Routine and office duties	
-	28.2.18		Inspected Mange cases in No. 1 Coy Train. Examined new premises for 43 D.V.S. Routine and office duties.	

M. Farnell Major A.V.C.
D.A.D.V.S. 33 Division

WAR DIARY or INTELLIGENCE SUMMARY

Army Form C. 2118.

D.D.V.S. 33 Division

Vol 29

Place	Date	Hour	Summary of Events and Information	Remarks and references to Appendices
H Field	1.3.19		Inspected new entrance of V.O. 33 Division. Inspected animals of 33 Divisional Head Quarters.	JHF
—	2.3.19		Attended conference of D.A.D.V.S. held at D.D.V.S. office 52 Corps Headquarters Lesdain	JHF
—	3.3.19		animals of N:1 Cy 33 Divisional Train. Latrine and office duties	JHF
—	4.3.19		Inspected mange cases in "B" Battery 162 Brigade R.F.A. Visited men pits prepared for H.M. Cattle Veterinary Section. Latrine and office duties	JHF
—	5.3.19		Inspected animals of 9th & 10th Brigade A.Q. 5th & 7th Kings Liverpool Regt, 2nd A & 7th Bty. 18 Ville	JHF
—	6.3.19		Air left 10th & 11th by 10th R.F.F.A. and 2nd machine Regt.	JHF
—	7.3.19		Inspected animals of 112 Brigade R.F.A. Latrin and office duties	JHF
—	8.3.19		Inspected animals of 156 Brigade R.F.A. Latrine and office duties	JHF
—	9.3.19		Inspected animals of 99th Inst. J. Ordnance and Dury cases in Ni Cy 33 Div Train	JHF
—	10.3.19		Latrine and office duties. Inspected left half Battalion Machine Gun Cy	JHF
—	11.3.19		Visited new entrance of V.O. 33 Division. Inspected animals of N:1 Section 33 D.A.C.	JHF
—	12.3.19		D.D.V.S. Fourth Army. Latrine and office duties	JHF
—	13.3.19		Inspected animals of 19th Infantry Brigade. Latrine and office duties	JHF
—	14.3.19		Inspected "A" Battery 156 Brigade R.F.A and 33 Signal Cy. P.E. Latrine and office duties	JHF

WAR DIARY or INTELLIGENCE SUMMARY

Army Form C. 2118.

War Diary of Capt. J.H. Farrell A.V.C. D.A.D.V.S. 33rd Division

Place	Date	Hour	Summary of Events and Information	Remarks and references to Appendices
In Field	12.3.18		Inspected animals of 11th I. Coy R.E. and 33 D.A.C. Routine and office duties.	JHF
"	13.3.18		Inspected animals of 33 Divisional Train, "B" Battery 162 Brigade R.F.A. and No 1 Section 33 D.A.C. Routine and office duties.	JHF
"	14.3.18		Inspected animals of No 2 Section 33 D.A.C., "B" Echelon D.A.C. 33 Bn M.M.G. and 1st & 2nd Field Veterinary Section. Routine and office duties.	JHF
"	15.3.18		Inspected animals of 11st Batt Middlesex Regt and 1st & 2nd Ambulance. Routine and office duties.	JHF
"	16.3.18		Attended Conference of D.A.D.V.S. at A.D.V.S. office 1st Corps H.Q. Vicinity Lieu of N.I. Coy 33 Divisional Train. Routine and office duties.	JHF
"	17.3.18		Inspected animals of No. 2, 3, 4 Coy Divisional Train. Routine and office duties.	JHF
"	18.3.18		Remounts to for 33 Divisional Artillery. Routine and office duties.	JHF
"	19.3.18		Inspected animals of "B" Battery 162 Brigade R.F.A. Routine and office duties	JHF
"	20.3.18		Inspected animals of 33 Signal Coy R.E. and Left half Battalion Machine Gun Coy.	JHF
"	21.3.18		Attended Conference held by Director of Veterinary Services at A.B.F.E.C. Routine and office duties.	JHF
"	22.3.18		Inspected No 1 Coy Train and No 2 Section 33 D.A.C. Worked out expenses of N.O.S. 33 Division fell at own expense. Routine and office duties.	JHF

WAR DIARY or INTELLIGENCE SUMMARY

Army Form C. 2118.

Major E.H. Farrell MC
D.A.D.V.S. 33 Division

Place	Date	Hour	Summary of Events and Information	Remarks and references to Appendices
In the Field and Billets			Attended Inspection of D.A.D.V.S. at A.D.V.S. office Sa Combe H.Q. Routine and office duties	
"	25.3.18		Inspected 15th + 16.1 Brigade R.F.A. Routine and office duties	EHF
"	26.3.18		Inspected N° 2 – 3 – 4 Corps Lorries, 100th Infantry Brigade, 99 and 101st F. Ambulance	EHF
"	26.3.18		Inspected animals of 2nd Wiltshire Regt. and 11.T.12 Wood & Veterinary Section	EHF
"	27.3.18		Inspected animals of 33 D.H.Q. Routine and office duties	EHF
"	28.3.18		Inspected 19th Infantry Brigade and N° 2 Section 33 D.A.C. Routine and office duties	EHF
"	29.3.18		Inspected an Inspection of V.O.ts 33 Division. Inspected animals of N° 1 Coy Div Train. Routine and office duties	EHF
"	30.3.18		Attended Inspection of D.A.D.V.S. at 98 Inf Headquarters. Visited 98 Infantry Brigade Headquarters. Routine and office duties	EHF
"	31.3.18		Inspected animals of D.H.Q. + R.A. Headquarters. Routine and office duties	EHF

E.H. Farrell Major MC
D.A.D.V.S. 33 Division

WAR DIARY or INTELLIGENCE SUMMARY

Army Form C. 2118.

WAR DIARY of Major E. A. Farrell R.V.C. **D.A.D.V.S. 33 Division**

Vol 30

Place	Date	Hour	Summary of Events and Information	Remarks and references to Appendices
In the Field	1.4.18		Inspected animals of E.A.A. Section 33 D.A.C. and No 2 + 4 Coys 33 Div Train	EAF
"	2.4.18		Inspected 156 Brigade R.F.A. Visited lines of 33rd Mobile Veterinary Section.	EAF
"	3.4.18		Several Reinforcements on arrival, to Units of the Division. Inspected animals of 162 Brigade. R.T.O. Routine and office duties.	EAF
"	4.4.18		Inspected animals of Divisional Headquarters and 33 Mobile Veterinary Section.	EAF
"	5.4.18		Inspected area of employees of Veterinary Officers 33 Division. Inspected animals of 33 Coys.	EAF
"	6.4.18		Car R.T.O. Routine and office duties.	EAF
"	6.4.18		Attended Conference of D.A.D.V.S. at A.D.V.S. 1st Corps Headquarters. Office and H.3 Mobile Veterinary Section moved from BRANDHOEK to HAUTEVILLE.	EAF
"	7.4.18		Interviewed A.D.V.S. 17th Corps. Inspected animals of E.A.A. Section 33 D.A.C.	EAF
"	8.4.18		Inspected animals of 33 Div Headquarters and 33 Mobile Veterinary Section. Routine and office duties.	EAF
"	9.4.18		Inspected animals of 33 Signal Coy R.E. and 11th Wireless Services. Routine and office duties.	EAF
"	10.4.18		Inspected animals of 33 Div Bat. Machine Gun Colls, + 19th Field Ambulance	EAF
"	11.4.18		Office and 33rd Mobile Veterinary Section moved from HAUTEVILLE to CAESTRE. Routine and office duties.	EAF

WAR DIARY
or
INTELLIGENCE SUMMARY.
(Erase heading not required.)

Army Form C. 2118.

Major J H Farnell A.V.C.
D.A.D.V.S. 33 Division

Place	Date	Hour	Summary of Events and Information	Remarks and references to Appendices
HQ Field	12.4.18		Inspected animals of No 5 Mobile Veterinary Section and 33 D.H.Q. Routine and office duties.	JHF
"	13.4.18		Office and M.V.S. moved from CAESTRE to BOESCHEPE. Visited new site for M.V.S.	JHF
"	14.4.18		Inspected animals of 212th & 222 Field companies R.E. Routine and office duties.	JHF
"	15.4.18		Inspected animals of No 2 Coy Machine Gun Bn and 99th Field Ambulance.	JHF
"	16.4.18		Inspected animals of 33 Divisional Headquarters. Office and M.V.S. moved from BOESCHEPE	JHF
"			to ABEELE.	
"	17.4.18		Inspected animals of 111th Field Coy R.E. Routine and office duties. Office and M.V.S. moved	JHF
"			to ABEELE AERODROME.	
"	18.4.18		Inspected animals and lines of No 3 Mobile Veterinary Section. Ch. Officer and 33 D. H.Q.	JHF
"			Routine and office duties.	
"	19.4.18		Inspected 33 Signal Coy R.E. and No 2 Coy 33 Divisional Train. Routine and office duties.	JHF
"	20.4.18		Attended conference of D.A.D.V.S. at A.D.V.S. office at Lake Headquarters.	JHF
"	21.4.18		Office and M.V.S. moved from ABEELE AERODROME to REMIGOR 16 (Ok a 9.7.) No 5	JHF
"			Mob MVS (40.000) Routine and office duties.	
"	22.4.18		Inspected animals of 100th Infantry Brigade and 33 Signal Coy R.E.	JHF
"	23.4.18		Inspected animals and lines of 33 D. H.Q. and No 4 Coy 33 Div Train.	JHF

WAR DIARY Major J. H. Farrell AVC D.A.D.V.S. 33 Division
or
INTELLIGENCE SUMMARY.
(Erase heading not required.)

Army Form C. 2118.

Place	Date	Hour	Summary of Events and Information	Remarks and references to Appendices
In the Field	24.4.18		Inspected animals of No 2 + 3 Coys 33 Divisional Train and 43 Mobile Veterinary Section. Routine and office duties.	JHF
"	25.4.18		Inspected 98th Infantry Brigade and 101st Field Ambulance. Routine and office duties.	JHF
"	26.4.18		Inspected animals of 19th Infantry Brigade. Routine and office duties.	JHF
"	27.4.18		Visited lines of 43 Mobile Veterinary Section, and inspected animals of S.A.A. Section 33 D.A.C.	JHF
"	28.4.18		Inspected animals of 33 Divisional Head-quarters. Routine and office duties.	JHF
"	29.4.18		Visited lines of 43rd Mobile Veterinary Section. Routine and office duties.	JHF
"	30.4.18		Inspected animals and lines of 33 Signal Coy R.E. Routine and office duties.	JHF

J H Farrell Maj AVC
D.A.D.V.S. 33 Division

15

WAR DIARY of Major J.F. Farrell. A.V.C.
D.A.D.V.S. 33 Division

Army Form C. 2118.

INTELLIGENCE SUMMARY

(Erase heading not required.)

Place	Date	Hour	Summary of Events and Information	Remarks and references to Appendices
In the Field	1.5.18		Visited lines of 33. D.A.C. and No 3rd Mobile Veterinary Section. Office moved to BLARINGHEM	
"	2.5.18		Inspected animals of 33 Batt Machine Gun Corps, Hd. Qrs Div Train, and 33 Signal Coy Jg. Cantine and office duties.	
"	3.5.18		Office and No 3rd M.V.S. moved from BLARINGHEM to J.H.A.T.S. Sept 27. Cantine and office duties.	
"	4.5.18		Attended conference of D.A.D.V.S. at 22nd Corps Headquarters. Cantine and office duties	
"	5.5.18		Inspected animals of 33 D.H.Q., H.3 M.V.S. moved to K.18.d.2.6 Sept 27. Cantine and office duties.	
"	6.5.18		Inspected animals of 1st Batt Queens Regt and S.A.A. Section. 33 D.A.C. Cantine and office duties	
"	7.5.18		Inspected animals of H.3 M.V.S., and No 2-3-4 Coys 33 Div Train. Cantine and office duties	
"	8.5.18		Inspected animals of 9 F.A. Sanitary Brigade. Cantine and office duties	
"	9.5.18		Inspected animals under treatment at H.3 Mobile Veterinary Section.	
"	10.5.18		Inspected animals of D. & E. Batteries 162 Brigade R.F.A. Cantine and office duties	
"	11.5.18		attended conference of D.A.D.V.S. at 2½ Corps Head quarters. Cantine and office duties.	

WAR DIARY or INTELLIGENCE SUMMARY

Army Form C. 2118.

of Major E. J. Farrell A.V.C. D.A.D.V.S. 33 Division

(Erase heading not required.)

Instructions regarding War Diaries and Intelligence Summaries are contained in F.S. Regs., Part II. and the Staff Manual respectively. Title pages will be prepared in manuscript.

Place	Date	Hour	Summary of Events and Information	Remarks and references to Appendices
In Field	12.5.18		Inspected A & D. Batteries 162 Brigade R.F.A. Routine and office duties	
"	13.5.18		Inspected animals of 33 D. H.Q. and 33 M.V.S. Routine and office duties	
"	14.5.18		Inspected 33 Signal Coy R.E. Routine and office duties	
"	15.5.18		Inspected animals of 98th Infantry Brigade. Routine and office duties	
"	16.5.18		Inspected animals of 100th Infantry Brigade. Routine and office duties	
"	17.5.18		Visited lines of No. 2 Section 33rd D.A.C.	
"	18.5.18		Attended Conference at D.A.D.V.S. at 1st Corps Head-quarters. Inspected animals of No. 2 and 3 Coys Divl Train, and 33 M.V.S. Routine and office duties	
"	19.5.18		Inspected animals of No. 1 Coy 33 Divl Train. Routine and office duties	
"	20.5.18		Inspected animals of 99th F. Ambulance to 3 M.V.S. and No. 4 Coy Train	
"	21.5.18		Inspected 19th & by Brigade, 11th Middlesex Pioneers, 19th and 99th F. Ambulance	
"	22.5.18		Inspected 33 Divl Machine Gun Battalion 11th, 212th and 222 Coys. R.E.	
"	23.5.18		Inspected animals of 33 M.V.S. and 33 D. H.Q. units. Routine and office duties	
"	24.5.18		Visited lines of 33 Signal Coy R.E. Routine and office duties	
"	25.5.18		Office work from I.D.M.A.V.W. to G.T.G.B.S. Met 2/7 Routine and office duties	
"	26.5.18		Attended Conference at 2nd Corps Head-quarters. Routine and office duties	

WAR DIARY of Major J. H. Farrell A.V.C
of
INTELLIGENCE SUMMARY. D.A.D.V.S. 33 Division
(Erase heading not required.)

Army Form C. 2118.

Place	Date	Hour	Summary of Events and Information	Remarks and references to Appendices
In the Field	27.5.18		Inspected 156 Brigade R.F.A. Routine and office duties	J.H.F.
"	28.5.18		Moved over Defences of V.O's, 33 Division. Routine and office duties.	J.H.F.
"	29.5.18		Inspected animals of 6.A.A. Section, 33 D.A.C., and visited Lines of 33 Signal Coy. R.E. and 33 D.H.Q.	J.H.F.
"	30.5.18		Attended office of A.D.V.S. 2nd Corps. Inspected animals of 99th F. Ambulance	J.H.F.
"	31.5.18		Inspected animals of No. 4 Coy 33 Div. Train. Routine and office duties.	J.H.F.

J.H.Farrell Major
D.A.D.V.S. 33 Division

WAR DIARY or INTELLIGENCE SUMMARY

Army Form C. 2118.

D.A.D.V.S. 33 Division of Maj. J.H. Farrell A.V.C.

Vol 32

Place	Date	Hour	Summary of Events and Information	Remarks and references to Appendices
Ed Zell	1.6.18		Inspected animals and lines of 142 Brigade R.F.A. and No 2 Section 33 D.A.C. Routine and office duties	J.H.F.
"	2.6.18		Inspected animals and lines of 33 Divisional Train. Routine and office duties	J.H.F.
"	3.6.18		Visited lines of 33 Divisional Headquarters and 33 Signal Coy R.E. Routine and office duties	J.H.F.
"	4.6.18		Attended Conference of D.A.D.V.S. at A.D.V.S. office. 2nd Army Headquarters. Inspected animals and lines of 3rd Mobile Veterinary Section. Routine and office duties	J.H.F.
"	5.6.18		Inspected animals of 33 Batt. Machine Gun Corps and No 1 Section 33 D.A.C. Routine and office duties	J.H.F.
"	6.6.18		Inspected animals of 19th Infantry Brigade and 18th Batt. Middlesex (Pioneers) Bn. Routine and office duties	J.H.F.
"	7.6.18		Inspected animals and lines of 33 Divisional Headquarters and 33 Signal Coy R.E. Routine and office duties	J.H.F.
"	8.6.18		Inspected animals and lines of 100th Inf. Brigade. Nos. 2, 3 and 4 Coys 33 Div. Train and 3rd Mobile Veterinary Section	J.H.F.
"	9.6.18		Attended office of A.D.V.S. 2nd Army, on duty. Routine and office duties	J.H.F.

WAR DIARY of No 9 & 3 Jamtl AVC
INTELLIGENCE SUMMARY. D.A.D.V.S. 33 Division

Army Form C. 2118.

(Erase heading not required.)

Place	Date	Hour	Summary of Events and Information	Remarks and references to Appendices
In the Field	10.6.18		Inspected animals of 19th and 16.2 Brigade R.F.A. Routine and office duties	[sgd]
"	11.6.18		Inspected animals and Lines of 33 Divisional Headquarters, 33 Signal Coy R.E. and B and C Batteries 162 Brigade R.F.A. Routine and office duties	[sgd]
"	12.6.18		Inspected animals of No 1 Coy Train and No 3 Mobile Veterinary Section. Routine and office duties.	[sgd]
"	13.6.18		Presided over a conference of Veterinary Officers, 33 Division. Routine and office duties	[sgd]
"	14.6.18		Inspected animals and Lines of 9th & 11th Brigade. Routine and office duties	[sgd]
"	15.6.18		Attended Conference of D.A.D.V.S. at A.D.V.S. 2nd Corps Headquarters.	[sgd]
"	16.6.18		Visited Lines of No 3 Mobile Veterinary Section and No 2 Section 33 D.A.C.	[sgd]
"	17.6.18		Inspected 11th, 12th, 222nd & Coys R.E. Routine and office duties	[sgd]
"	18.6.18		Inspected animals and Lines of No 1 Section 33 D.A.C. Routine and office duties	[sgd]
"	19.6.18		Routine and office duties	[sgd]
"	20.6.18		Inspected animals of 162 Brigade and A + B Batteries 156 Brigade R.F.A.	[sgd]
"	21.6.18		Inspected animals and lines of No 3 and 4 Coys 33 Div Train and 33 Div. V.S.	[sgd]
"	22.6.18		Inspected animals of 10th, 99th, and 100th & Ambulances. Routine and office duties.	[sgd]

WAR DIARY
INTELLIGENCE SUMMARY. of A.D.V.S. 33 Division

Army Form C. 2118.

Place	Date	Hour	Summary of Events and Information	Remarks and references to Appendices
In the Field	23.6.19		Inspected animals and lines of 16t Brigade R.F.A Routine and office duties	J.F.
"	24.6.19		Inspected animals of S.A.A Section 33 D.A.C, 4-2 M.V.S and 33 Signal Co Y.S	J.F.
"	25.6.19		Inspected animals of N.1 Section 33 D.A.C and visited 42 M.V.S also conducted animals awaiting purchase for R.A. Horse being despatched to Base Remounts	J.F.
"	26.6.19		Attended Conference of D.A.D.V.S. at A.D.V.S office 2nd Corps Headquarters. Inspected animals of 33 Divisional Headquarters. Routine and office duties	J.F.
"	27.6.19		Inspected animals of N.1 Section 33 D.A.C, N.1 Coy Train and 4-3 M.V.S. Routine and office duties	J.F.
"	28.6.19		Attended Conference at A.D.V.S office 2nd Corps Headquarters. Routine and office duties	J.F.
"	29.6.19		Inspected and conferences of Veterinary Officers. 33 Division Routine and office duties	J.F.
"	30.6.19		Inspected animals of 33 D.H.Q and 33 Signal Coy R.E. Routine and office duties	J.F.

J. Farrell Major
D.A.D.V.S. 33 Division

WAR DIARY of Major J. F. Farrell A.V.C. D.A.D.V.S. 33 Division
INTELLIGENCE SUMMARY

Army Form C. 2118.

Place	Date	Hour	Summary of Events and Information	Remarks and references to Appendices
In the Field	1.7.18		Inspected animals and lines of 33 Divisional Headquarters and 33 Signal Coy. R.E. Routine and office duties.	J.F.F.
"	2.7.18		Inspected animals of N.3 Mobile Veterinary Section and N.M.P., 33 Division. Routine and office duties.	J.F.F.
"	3.7.18		Inspected animals and lines of 19th Infantry Brigade. Routine and office duties.	J.F.F.
"	4.7.18		Inspected animals of 156 Brigade R.F.A. and No. 2 Section 33 D.A.C. Routine and office duties.	J.F.F.
"	5.7.18		Inspected animals of 11th, 212th and 222nd I. Coys R.E. and 100th Infantry Brigade. Routine and office duties.	J.F.F.
"	6.7.18		Inspected N.3 Mobile Veterinary Section, No. 1, 2 and 3 Coys Div Train and 33 Signal Coy R.E. Routine and office duties.	J.F.F.
"	7.7.18		Inspected animals of 162 Brigade R.F.A. Routine and office duties.	J.F.F.
"	8.7.18		Attended office of A.D.V.S. 2nd Corps, and visited lines of 33 Div. Headquarters. Routine and office duties.	J.F.F.
"	9.7.18		Visited on Inference of Veterinary Officers, 33 Division. Inspected animals of L.A.A. Section 33 D.A.C. Routine and office duties.	J.F.F.

WAR DIARY of Major E. F. Farrell A.V.C. D.A.D.V.S.
or
INTELLIGENCE SUMMARY. 33rd Division

Army Form C. 2118.

(Erase heading not required.)

Place	Date	Hour	Summary of Events and Information	Remarks and references to Appendices
In the Field	10.7.18		Inspected animals and lines of 19th, 99th, and 101st F. Ambulances. Routine and office duties	E.F.F.
"	11.7.18		Inspected 98th Infantry Brigade and 19th Middlesex (Pioneer) Regt. Routine and office duties.	E.F.F.
"	12.7.18		Inspected animals of 33 Div. Headquarters. Routine and office duties	E.F.F.
"	13.7.18		Inspected animals of No. 1 Section 33 D.A.C.	
"	14.7.18		Visited lines of No. 3 Mobile Veterinary Section and inspected animals of 33 Int. Vickers Gun Corps. Routine and office duties.	E.F.F.
"	15.7.18		Inspected animals of 156 Brigade R.F.A. and No. 1 Section 33 D.A.C., also pick lines of each Battery	E.F.F.
"	16.7.18		Inspected 162 Brigade R.F.A and No. 2 Section 33 D.A.C., also pick lines of each Battery and D.A.C. Routine and office duties	E.F.F.
"	17.7.18		Inspected animals of No. 3 Mobile Veterinary Section, and No. 1 and No. Supp 33 tri Train. Routine and office duties	E.F.F.
"	18.7.18		Inspected animals of 98th and 100th Inf. Brigade. Routine and office duties	E.F.F.
"	19.7.18		Inspected No. 2 and 3 Supp Train and visited lines of A.D.V.S.	E.F.F.
"	20.7.18		Inspected animals of No. 1 and 2 Section 33 D.A.C. Routine and office duties	E.F.F.
"	21.7.18		Attended Conference at D.A.D.V.S. at 2nd Corps Headquarters. Inspected 2.2 and 2.2.2 Emp. F.C.	E.F.F.

Army Form C. 2118.

WAR DIARY of Major E. F. Farrell A.V.C.
INTELLIGENCE SUMMARY D.A.D.V.S.
33 Division

(Erase heading not required.)

Place	Date	Hour	Summary of Events and Information	Remarks and references to Appendices
In the Field	22.7.18		Inspected animals of 100th Inf. Brigade, 11th F. Coy. R.E., and 6. A.A. Section 33 D.A.C.	JHF
"	23.7.18		Routine and office duties	
"			Inspected 10th, 99th and 101st F. Ambulance. Visited lines of 4.3 M.V.S. Routine and office duties	JHF
"	24.7.18		Presided over a Conference of Veterinary Officers, 33 Division. Inspected animals of 33 Bn Machine gun Corps. Routine and office duties	JHF
"	25.7.18		Inspected animals of 162 Brigade R.F.A. Routine and office duties	JHF
"	26.7.18		Inspected 33 Div Train and 4.3 Mobile Veterinary Section. Routine and office duties	JHF
"	27.7.18		Accompanied A.D.V.S. 2nd Corps on inspection of 6.A.A. Section D.A.C., 9 F.C. Inf. Brigade,	JHF
"			10/156 Brigade, "C" Battery 162 Brigade R.F.A., and 33 Bn Machine gun Corps.	JHF
"	28.7.18		Inspected "A", "B", and "C" Batteries 156 Brigade R.F.A., and 19th Infantry Brigade. Routine and office duties	JHF
"	29.7.18		Inspected animals of "A", "B" and "D" Batteries 162 Bde R.F.A. Routine and office duties	JHF
"	30.7.18		Attended office of A.D.V.S. 1st Corps. Routine and office duties	JHF
"	31.7.18		Inspected animals of 9 F.C. Inf. Brigade and 4.3 D.V.S. Routine and office duties	JHF

J H Farrell Major
D.A.D.V.S.
33 Division

Army Form C. 2118.

WAR DIARY of Major E. H. Farrell. A.V.C.
or
INTELLIGENCE SUMMARY. D.A.D.V.S.
33 Division
(Erase heading not required.)

WO 34

Place	Date	Hour	Summary of Events and Information	Remarks and references to Appendices
In the Field	1.8.18		Inspected animals of "B" and "D" Batteries 156 Brigade R.F.A. "A" Battery 162 Brigade and No.1 and 2 Sections 33 D.A.C. Routine and office duties.	EHF
"	2.8.18		Attended office of A.D.V.S. 2nd Corps and inspected animals and Corps of L.3 Mobile Veterinary Section. Routine and office duties.	EHF
"	3.8.18		Inspected animals of 33 Divisional Train. Routine and office duties.	EHF
"	4.8.18		Attended Conference of D.A.D.V.S. at 2nd Corps Headquarters. Inspected animals of 156 & 36 R.F.A. Routine and office duties.	EHF
"	5.8.18		Inspected personnel on parade at L.3 M.V.S. Routine and office duties.	EHF
"	6.8.18		Lining the route of King escorted to His Majesty the King. Presided over Conference of Veterinary Officers 33 Division. Attended office of A.D.V.S. 2nd Corps. Routine and office duties.	EHF
"	7.8.18		Inspected animals of 162 Brigade R.F.A. Routine and office duties.	EHF
"	8.8.18		Inspected animals of 11- 212 and 222, I. Coy. R.E., 33 Div M.M.P. and D.N.G.	EHF
"	9.8.18		Inspected 33 Signal Coy. R.E. and L.3 M.V.S. Routine and office duties.	EHF
"	10.8.18		Visited No. 2. Veterinary Evacuation Station and inspected animals of 19-99 and 100th I. Ambulances. Routine and office duties.	EHF
"	11.8.18		Inspected animals of 100th Inf. Brigade, 33 Bn. Machine Gun Corps and L.A. Section D.A.C.	EHF

(A9475) Wt W358/P560 600,000 12/17 D.D. & L. Sch. 82a. Forms/C2118/15.

Army Form C. 2118.

WAR DIARY of Maj. E.J. Farrell A.V.C. D.A.D.V.S. 33 Division
INTELLIGENCE SUMMARY
(Erase heading not required.)

Instructions regarding War Diaries and Intelligence Summaries are contained in F.S. Regs., Part II. and the Staff Manual respectively. Title pages will be prepared in manuscript.

Place	Date	Hour	Summary of Events and Information	Remarks and references to Appendices
In the Field	1.8.18		Inspected animals of 15th Inf. Brigade, and visited Lines of 4.3 M.V.S. Routine and office duties.	EJF
"	13.8.18		Inspected animals of 19th Inf. Brigade. Routine and office duties.	EJF
"	14.8.18		Inspected 33 Signal Coy R.E. and 4.3 M.V.S. Routine and office duties	EJF
"	15.8.18		Inspected Animals of 156 Brigade R.F.A. and No.1 Section 33 D.A.C.	EJF
"	16.8.18		Inspected Animals of 33 D.H.Q. and No.2 Section 33 D.A.C. Routine and office duties	EJF
"	17.8.18		Inspected animals of 156 and 162 Brigades R.F.A. Routine and office duties	EJF
"	18.8.18		Inspected O.R. and M.O. Inf. Brigades, Z.A.A. Section D.A.C., and 4.3 M.V.S. Routine and office duties.	EJF
"	19.8.18		Presided over Conference of Veterinary Officers, 33 Division. Routine and office duties.	EJF
"	20.8.18		Moved from 2.17 - F.22. Located at EPLECQUES. Visited Lines of 33 D.H.Q.	EJF
"	21.8.18		Routine and office duties.	EJF
"	22.8.18		Inspected animals and lines of 4.3 M.V.S. Routine and office duties	EJF
"	23.8.18		Attended inspection of 6 A.A. Section 33 D.A.C. by A.D.V.S. 7th Corps.	EJF
"	24.8.18		Attended conference at D.A.D.V.S. of 7th Corps. Headquarters. Routine and office duties	EJF

WAR DIARY of Naj. & F. Farrell A.V.C.
or
INTELLIGENCE SUMMARY. D.A.D.V.S.
33 Division

Army Form C. 2118.

Place	Date	Hour	Summary of Events and Information	Remarks and references to Appendices
In the Field	24.8.18		Inspected animals of D.H.Q, 33 Signal Coy R.E. and 4.3 N.Y.B. Routine and office duties	E.H.
"	25.8.18		Inspected 98th Lt Brigade and 90th F. Ambulance. Routine and office duties	E.H.
"	26.8.18		Attended office of A.D.V.S. no horses for duty. Inspected 33 Signal Coy R.E.	E.H.
"	27.8.18		Inspected animals of 33 Bn Machine Gun Corps & 33 D.H.Q. Routine and office duties	E.H.
"	28.8.18		Moved from EPERLECQUES to SAULTY. Routine and office duties	E.H.
"	29.8.18		Attended office of A.D.V.S. 17th horse Inspected animals of 4.3 N.Y.B. Routine and office duties	E.H.
"	30.8.18		Inspected animals of 19.98.100 & Lt Brigades and 33 Div Train Routine & office duties	E.H.
"	31.8.18		Inspected animals of 4.3 N.Y.B., 33 D.H.Q. & 33 Signal Coy R.E. Routine and office duties	E.H.

J. Farrell Maj.
D.A.D.V.S.
33 Division

WAR DIARY of Majr G. N. Fanell. A.V.C.
INTELLIGENCE SUMMARY. D.A.D.V.S. 33 Division

Army Form C. 2118.

14

Instructions regarding War Diaries and Intelligence Summaries are contained in F. S. Regs., Part II. and the Staff Manual respectively. Title pages will be prepared in manuscript.

(Erase heading not required.)

Vol 35

Place	Date	Hour	Summary of Events and Information	Remarks and references to Appendices
In the Field	1.9.18		Inspected animals and lines of 19th F. Ambulance. Routine and office duties.	
"	2.9.18		Inspected animals of 33 D.N.Q. and 4 D.N.V.S. Condition of animals good. Routine and office duties.	
"	3.9.18		Inspected animals of 162 Brigade R.F.A. General condition good. Routine and office duties.	
"	4.9.18		Office and 4.D N.V.S. moved from SAULTY to LUCHEUX. Routine and office duties.	
"	5.9.18		Inspected animals of 156 Brigade R.F.A., 19th Inf. Brigade and 19th F. Ambulance.	
"	6.9.18		Routine and office duties.	
"	7.9.18		Proceeded on 14 days leave to UNITED KINGDOM. Capt. A. E. Cahn A.V.C., O.C. 4 D.N.V.S. appointed to take over my duties during my absence.	

Army Form C. 2118.

WAR DIARY of Capt. A.G. Cater A.V.C.
or
INTELLIGENCE SUMMARY. A/D.A.D.V.S. 33 Division

(Erase heading not required.)

Instructions regarding War Diaries and Intelligence Summaries are contained in F. S. Regs., Part II. and the Staff Manual respectively. Title pages will be prepared in manuscript.

Place	Date	Hour	Summary of Events and Information	Remarks and references to Appendices
In the Field	8.9.18		Inspected animals of 33 Divisional Headquarters. Presided over presence of veterinary officers	
"	9.9.18		33 Division. Routine and office duties	
"	10.9.18		Inspected animals of 10th Infantry Brigade. Routine and office duties	
"	11.9.18		Inspected animals of 33 Battalion Machine gun Corps. Routine and office duties	
"	12.9.18		Routine and office duties	
"	13.9.18		Inspected animals of 10th F. Ambulance, 1st Batt. Queens Regt and 1st Batt. Cameronians. Routine and office duties	
"	14.9.18		Inspected animals of 33rd Signal Coy R.E. and 33 D.N.Q. Units. Routine and office duties	
"	15.9.18		Routine and office duties	
"	16.9.18		Office and A.D.V.S. moved from LUCHEUX to LE BOUFF.	
"	17.9.18		Routine and office duties	
"	18.9.18		Inspected animals of 9th Infantry Brigade. Routine and office duties	
"	19.9.18		Inspected wounded animals of 18th Batt. Middlesex (Pioneers) Regt. Routine and office duties	
"	20.9.18		Inspected animals of 11th F. Coy R.E. and 33 Signal Coy R.E. Routine and office duties	
"	21.9.18		Inspected animals of 10th Infantry Brigade. Routine and office duties	

WAR DIARY of Lat A.V.C. Col A.V.C. **Army Form C. 2118.**

or

INTELLIGENCE SUMMARY. A/ D.A.D.V.S.
33 Division

(Erase heading not required.)

Instructions regarding War Diaries and Intelligence Summaries are contained in F. S. Regs., Part II. and the Staff Manual respectively. Title pages will be prepared in manuscript.

Place	Date	Hour	Summary of Events and Information	Remarks and references to Appendices
In the Field	22.9.18		Inspected animals of S.A.A. Section 33 D.A.C., 18th Batt. Middlesex Regt. and 33 Signal Coy. P.C. Routine and office duties	
"	23.9.18		Inspected animals of 33 Batt. Machine Gun Corps. Routine and office duties	
"	24.9.18		L.S.M.V.S. moved from O.33.b.3.8. to V.G.a.a.9. Sheet 27C. Routine and office duties	
"	25.9.18		Inspected Suspected Itematics cases in D/162 Brigade R.F.A. and animals of the 13 attery. Routine and office duties. Notification received to the effect that Major G. T. Farrell A.V.C., D.A.D.V.S. 33 Division had been granted 14 days extension of leave from France, on Medical Certificate. (Authority War Office letter No. 100/Veterinary 39 (V.D.) dated 19th Sept. 1918.	
"	26.9.18		Inspected animals of 5th Scottish Rifles, 11th F. Coy. R.E., and 1/9th Bat N.F. Routine and office duties	
"	27.9.18		Inspected new advanced site for A.D.M.V.S. in view of an early move. Inspected animals and lines of 33 Batt. Machine Gun Corps. Routine and office duties	
"	28.9.18		Attended Conference of A.D.V.S. at A.D.V.S. office VA b/o Headquarters	
"	29.9.18		Inspected animals of 1st Batt. Queens Regt. 1st Gameronians and Nos. 1, 2 and 3 Coy. Train	

WAR DIARY of Capt A.E. Cator A.V.C.

INTELLIGENCE SUMMARY. a/ D.A.D.V.S. 33 Division

Army Form C. 2118.

(Erase heading not required.)

Place	Date	Hour	Summary of Events and Information	Remarks and references to Appendices
In the Field	30.9.18		Inspected animals of 33 Signal Coy R.E., 33 D. H.Q and animals assembled by shell fire in 11th F. Coy R.E. Routine and office duties.	

C.B. Lobb
Capt. A.V.C.
a/ D.A.D.V.S.
33 Division

Army Form C. 2118.

WAR DIARY of Capt. A.E.Cato.A.V.C.
INTELLIGENCE SUMMARY. A/D.A.D.V.S.
33 Division

(Erase heading not required.)

Place	Date	Hour	Summary of Events and Information	Remarks and references to Appendices
In the Field	1.10.18		Inspected Transport Lines and making arrangements of 98th and 100th Infantry Brigades. Routine and office duties.	EAC.
"	2.10.18		Inspected lines of 156 Brigade R.F.A and 19th Inf Brigade. Routine and office duties.	EAC.
"	3.10.18		Visited lines of 33 Div Train. Routine and office duties.	EAC.
"	4.10.18		Inspected animals of 156 Brigade R.F.A. Routine and office duties	EAC.
"	5.10.18		Inspected animals of 162 Brigade R.F.A. Routine and office duties	EAC.
"	6.10.18		Inspected animals of 33 Div Headquarters and 33 Signal Coy. R.E.	EAC.

Army Form C. 2118.

WAR DIARY of Major E. J. Farrell, A.V.C.
of
INTELLIGENCE SUMMARY. D.A.D.V.S. 33 Division

(Erase heading not required.)

Place	Date	Hour	Summary of Events and Information	Remarks and references to Appendices
In the Field	7.10.18		Returned from leave and took over duties of D.A.D.V.S. Division	JF
"	8.10.18		Inspected animals of 33 Batt. Machine gun Corps and 19th F. Ambulance. Routine and office duties	JF
"	9.10.18		Inspected animals of 99 and 100th F. Ambulances. Visited lines of 4.3 M.V.S. Routine and office duties.	JF
"	10.10.18		Inspected animals of 33 Div Headquarters and 33 Signal Coy. P.O. Routine and office duties.	JF
"	11.10.18		Visited lines of 4.3 M. Mobile Veterinary Section and inspected 1/4th Batt. Kings (Liverpool Reg)	JF
"	12.10.18		Routine and office duties.	JF
"	13.10.18		Inspected animals of 19th Infantry Brigade. Routine and office duties.	JF
"	14.10.18		Inspected animals of 91st Infantry Brigade. Routine and office duties.	JF
"	15.10.18		Inspected animals of L.A.A. Section 33 D.A.C. and 33 Signal Coy R.E. Routine and office duties.	JF
"	16.10.18		Inspected animals of 33 D.A.C., 4.3 M.V.S., and 33 Div Headquarters. Routine and office duties.	JF
"	17.10.18		Inspected animals of 100th Infantry Brigade. Routine and office duties.	JF
"	18.10.18		Inspected animals of G.O.C. 33 Division. Inspected animals of 1/6 Brigade R.F.A. Routine and office duties.	JF

Army Form C. 2118.

WAR DIARY of Maj. E. J. N. Farrell, A.V.C.
or
INTELLIGENCE SUMMARY. D.A.D.V.S.
33 Division

Instructions regarding War Diaries and Intelligence Summaries are contained in F.S. Regs., Part II. and the Staff Manual respectively. Title pages will be prepared in manuscript.

(Erase heading not required.)

Place	Date	Hour	Summary of Events and Information	Remarks and references to Appendices
In the Field	18.10.18		Inspected animals of 162 Brigade R.F.A. Parties and office duties	J.H.T.
"	19.10.18		Inspected animals of 11-212. 222 F. Coys. P.C. Parties and office duties	J.H.T.
"	20.10.18		Attended office of A.D.V.S. V. Corps (holi) and inspected 99 F. Ambulance and No. 2 + 3 Cav. Train.	J.H.T.
"	21.10.18		Inspected animals of 33 Div. Headquarters and 43 N.V.S. Parties and office duties	J.H.T.
"	22.10.18		Office moved from ELARY to TROISVILLES P.T. Parties and office duties.	J.H.T.
"	23.10.18		Visited No. 5 Veterinary Evacuation Station. Inspected 33 Signal Coy P.C.	J.H.T.
"	24.10.18		Office moved from TROISVILLES to FOREST. Parties and office duties.	J.H.T.
"	25.10.18		Office moved from FOREST to TROISVILLES P.T. Parties and office duties.	J.H.T.
"	26.10.18		Inspected animals and horses at 43 N.V.S. Parties and office duties	J.H.T.
"	27.10.18		Inspected animals of 33 Div. Headquarters. Parties and other duties	J.H.T.
"	28.10.18		Inspected animals of No. 16 Coy 33 Div. Train. Parties and office duties	J.H.T.
"	29.10.18		Inspected 33 Batt. Machine Gun Corps and D.H.Q. units. Parties and office duties	J.H.T.
"	30.11.18		Inspected animals of 19th Infantry Brigade. Parties and office duties	J.H.T.
"	31.10.18		Inspected animals of 156 Brigade R.F.A. and No. 1 See D.A.C.	J.H.T.

E. J. N. Farrell
D.A.D.V.S.
33 Div.

WAR DIARY of Major E. H. Farrell, M.R.C
INTELLIGENCE SUMMARY. D.A.D.V.S.
33 Division

Army Form C. 2118.

Vol. 38

Place	Date	Hour	Summary of Events and Information	Remarks and references to Appendices
In the Field	1.11.18		Inspected Animals of 33 Divisional Headquarters, 33 Div Signal Coy. R.E., and all S.A.A. awaiting evacuation at 1 & 3rd Mobile Veterinary Section. Parties and office duties	
"	2.11.18		Inspected Remounts issued to 33 Bat. Machine Gun Bn/o and all animals of S.A.A. Section 33. D.A.C. Parties and office duties.	
"	3.11.18		Inspected animals of 95th and 100th Infantry Brigades and 11th Bn Middlesex Regiment	
"	4.11.18		Office moved from TROISVILLES to FORÊT. Parties and office duties.	
"	5.11.18		Office moved from FORÊT to ENGLEFONTAINE. Parties and office duties.	
"	6.11.18		Moved from ENGLEFONTAINE to SARS BAS (I.6.b.6.0 Sheet 57A). Parties and office duties	
"	7.11.18		Inspected animals and lines of 33 Bn. Machine Gun Bn/o. Parties and office duties.	
"	8.11.18		Inspected all animals of 33 Div Train, 43 N. V.S., and S.A.A. See D.A.C.	
"	9.11.18		Inspected animals of 100th Infantry Brigade and 33 Signal Coy R.E. Parties and office duties.	
"	10.11.18		Attended Conference of D.A.D.V.S at V & N.D Headquarters. Inspected Animals of 15th Brigade R.F.A. Parties and office duties	
"	11.11.18		Inspected animals and lines of 43 N. V.S. Parties and office duties.	
"	12.11.18		Office moved from SARS BAS to BERLAIMONT. Parties and office duties.	
"	13.11.18		Inspected animals of 100th Infantry Brigade. Parties and office duties.	

Army Form C. 2118.

WAR DIARY of No 5 C.F. Jaun. A.D.C
or
INTELLIGENCE SUMMARY. D.A.D.V.S.
33 Division

(Erase heading not required.)

Place	Date	Hour	Summary of Events and Information	Remarks and references to Appendices
Ch. Bel.	14.11.18		Inspected STOMATITIS cases in 2nd Batt Worcester Regt. Panties and office duties	C.H.H
"	15.11.18		Inspected L.S.A. Sec D.A.C. and 10 F. Ambulance. Panties and office duties	C.H.H
"	16.11.18		Office moved from BERLHIMONT to MONTIGNY. Panties and office duties	C.H.H
"	17.11.18		Inspected 19th Cav Brigade, 2nd Batt A.P.L.H. and 99. 1 mtd F. Ambulance.	C.H.H
"	18.11.18		Inspected 11. 212. 222. F. Coys. R.E. and 43 M.V.S. Panties and Office duties.	C.H.H
"	19.11.18		Inspected 98th and 100th Cav Brigade. Panties and office duties.	C.H.H
"	20.11.18		Inspected 19th Cav Brigade and 33 D.F.O units. Panties and office duties	C.H.H
"	21.11.18		Inspected 15th Brigade and N° 1 Sec 33.D.A.C. Panties and office duties	C.H.H
"	22.11.18		Inspected 162 Brigade and N° 1 Sec 33 D.A.C. Panties and office duties	C.H.H
"	23.11.18		Inspected N° 2 Cav Train, 43 M.V.S. and 33 Divisl Cav P.C. Panties and office duties.	C.H.H
"	24.11.18		Inspected animals of 99. 1 mtd F. Ambulances. Panties and office duties	C.H.H
"	25.11.18		Inspected 162 Brigade R.F.A. and N° 2 Section D.A.C. Panties and office duties	C.H.H
"	26.11.18		Inspected 98th Cav Brigade and 112. F Cav P.C. Panties and office duties	C.H.H
"	27.11.18		Visited units of 43 M.V.S. Panties and office duties	C.H.H
"	28.11.18		Inspected animals of 33 Div Headquarters and N° 4 Cav Train.	C.H.H
"	29.11.18		Inspected Animals of 100th Cav Brigade and 19th F. Ambulance.	C.H.H

Army Form C. 2118.

WAR DIARY of No/S.C. Harvell A.D.C
INTELLIGENCE SUMMARY. D.A.D.V.S. 33 Div

(Erase heading not required.)

Place	Date	Hour	Summary of Events and Information	Remarks and references to Appendices
In the Field	30.11.18		Completed arrivals of 33 Separal Cav P.C. Lautes and officer duties	

J.H.Harvell Maj
D.A.D.V.S.
33 Division

WAR DIARY
INTELLIGENCE SUMMARY

Army Form C. 2118.

N°1 C. H. Farrell, D.A.V.C.
D.A.V.S. 33 Division

Place	Date	Hour	Summary of Events and Information	Remarks and references to Appendices
In the Field	1.12.18		Assisted new Inspector of Veterinary Officers 33 Division. Parties & office duties.	CHF
"	2.12.18		Inspected animals of 33 Divisional Headquarters and 33 Light Inf. P.C.	CHF
"	3.12.18		Visited kits of 4.3 N.V.S. and inspected all 2 & 9 animals awaiting evacuation	CHF
"	4.12.18		Inspected 19th Brigade R.F.A. and N°1 Section 33 D.A.C.	CHF
"	5.12.18		Inspected 162 Brigade R.F.A. and N°2 Section 33 D.A.C.	CHF
"	6.12.18		Arrival evacuation of army Mors at NINTIGNY.	CHF
"	7.12.18		Inspected animals of S.A. & Zetters 33 D.A.C. and N°1 Amm Train	CHF
"	8.12.18		Inspected animals of 10th Infantry Brigade, and 11th L. Inf. P.C.	CHF
"	9.12.18		Parties and office duties	CHF
"	10.12.18		Parties and office duties	CHF
"	11.12.18		Moved from NINTIGNY to HORNOY.	CHF
"	12.12.18		Selected entraining site for 4.3 N Mobile Veterinary Section. Parties and office duties.	CHF
"	13.12.18		Visited lines of N.F.A. Brigade R.F.A.	CHF
"	14.12.18		Inspected area to be occupied by animals of this Division, on Conclusion of march.	CHF
"	15.12.18		Parties and office duties	CHF
"	16.12.18		Inspected animals of 33 Div Headquarters and L.B. N.V.S.	CHF

Army Form C. 2118.

WAR DIARY
or
INTELLIGENCE SUMMARY.

(Erase heading not required.)

War Diary of Nos. 6 & 7 Sects. 'A' M.T.
D.A.D.V.S.
33 Division

Instructions regarding War Diaries and Intelligence Summaries are contained in F.S. Regs., Part II. and the Staff Manual respectively. Title pages will be prepared in manuscript.

Place	Date	Hour	Summary of Events and Information	Remarks and references to Appendices
In the Field	17.12.18		Inspected animals of 33 Signal Coy R.E., and 7.O. Units	JHT
"	18.12.18		Inspected animals of 19th Infantry Brigade and No. 6 Coy Train	JHT
"	19.12.18		Visited lines of L.3 N.Y.S. and 101 F. Ambulance	JHT
"	20.12.18		Inspected 33 Batt. Machine Gun Corps and 222 Field Coy R.E.	JHT
"	21.12.18		Inspected animals of 9th Infantry Brigade and 99 F. Ambulance	JHT
"	22.12.18		Inspected animals and lines of 9th & 10th Infantry Brigade and 11th F. Coy R.E.	JHT
"	23.12.18		Individually examined all animals of 33 Div. Ambulance and M.V. Settie	JHT
"	24.12.18		Inspected animals awaiting evacuation at 4.3 N.Y.S.	JHT
"	25.12.18		Routine and office duties	JHT
"	26.12.18		Routine and office duties	JHT
"	27.12.18		Received no return of Veterinary Officers 33 Division	JHT
"	28.12.18		Inspected animals of 33 D.T.Q. Units for Demobilization	JHT
"	29.12.18		Inspected animals of 100th Infy. Brigade for Demobilization	JHT
"	30.12.18		Inspected animals of 33 Batt. Machine Gun Corps and 1st Batt. Middlesex Regt. for Demobilization	JHT
"	31.12.18		Inspected animals of 98th Infy. Brigade Group for Demobilization	JHT

J.H. Farrell Capt.
D.A.D.V.S.
33 Division

Army Form C. 2118.

WAR DIARY
or
INTELLIGENCE SUMMARY.
(Erase heading not required.)

A.D.V.S. 33rd DIVISION.

Place	Date	Hour	Summary of Events and Information	Remarks and references to Appendices
In the field	1.1.19		Routine and office duties	J.H.
"	2.1.19		Examination of animals for demobilization. Routine and office	J.H.
"	3.1.19		Routine and office duties	J.H.
"	4.1.19		Examination of animals for demobilization. Routine and office duties	J.H.
"	5.1.19		Routine and office duties	J.H.
"	6.1.19		Examination of animals for demobilization. Routine and office duties	J.H.
"	7.1.19		Routine and office duties	J.H.
"	8.1.19		Examination of animals for demobilization. Routine and office duties	J.H.
"	9.1.19		Routine and office duties	J.H.
"	10.1.19		Examination of animals for demobilization. Routine and office duties	J.H.
"	11.1.19		Routine and office duties	J.H.

WAR DIARY
or
INTELLIGENCE SUMMARY.

(Erase heading not required.)

Army Form. C. 2118.

G. Hannell Major RAMC
D.A.D.V.S. 3rd DIVISION.
33 Division

Date 5/2/19

Place	Date	Hour	Summary of Events and Information	Remarks and references to Appendices
L. McCall	12.1.19		Examination of animals for Ausstellung. Routine and office duties	
"	13.1.19		Office duties	
"	14.1.19		Moved to Cubervalle. Routine and office duties	
"	15.1.19		Moved to the Marguerite S. Routine and office duties	
"	16.1.19		Inspected animals at Headquarters. Routine and office duties	
"	17.1.19		Inspected animals of Signals. Routine and office duties	
"	18.1.19		Visited D.D.V.S. Routine and office duties	
"	19.1.19		Inspected No. 4 Company Drivers. Routine and office duties	
"	20.1.19		Inspected 2nd Howitzers. Routine and office duties	
"	21.1.19		Inspected 222nd Royal Engineers. Routine and office duties	
"	22.1.19		Inspected 9th K.R.L. Routine and office duties	
"	23.1.19		Inspected 16th K.R.R's. Routine and office duties	
"	24.1.19		Routine and office duties	
"	25.1.19		Mustering of horses of 33 D.H.Q. Routine and office duties	
"	25.1.19		Mustering of horses of 33 Signals R.E. Routine and office duties	
"	26.1.19		Routine and office duties	

Army Form C. 2118.

DIVISION. 33rd Division

WAR DIARY
or
INTELLIGENCE SUMMARY.

(Erase heading not required.)

Instructions regarding War Diaries and Intelligence Summaries are contained in F. S. Regs., Part II. and the Staff Manual respectively. Title pages will be prepared in manuscript.

Place	Date	Hour	Summary of Events and Information	Remarks and references to Appendices
In the Field	27.1.19		Routine and Office duties	
	28.1.19		Inspected 100th Inf. Bde. group. Routine and Office duties	
	29.1.19		Inspected 2nd Hussars, 16th R.W.S, A.S.S, his train, 222 R.E.s 10th & 9th Ambulances. Routine and Office duties	
	30.1.19		Inspected Horses of 33 Div. Signals. Routine and office duties	
	31.1.19		Office moved to Taragonville. Routine and office duties.	

Confidential

War Diary
of
DADVS 33rd Division
for
February 1919.

Original.

WAR DIARY
or
INTELLIGENCE SUMMARY.
(Erase heading not required.)

Army Form C. 2118.

Major RAVC
D.A.D.V.S. 33 Division

B.A.D.V.S.
33rd DIVISION.

Place	Date	Hour	Summary of Events and Information	Remarks and references to Appendices
In the field	1/2/19		Routine and office duties	
"	2/2/19		Routine and office duties	
"	3/2/19		Inspected animals of 100th Lgt Bde H.Q., Routine and office duties	
"	4/2/19		Inspected animals of 70th (Coy Train), 2nd Worcesters, 9th H.I., 16 K.R.R., 222 M.G and 33rd M.G.C. Routine and office duties	
"	5/2/19		Routine and office duties	
"	6/2/19		Inspected 7 animals of 100th Inf Bde Group before being sent to No. 9 Vet Hospital. Routine and office duties	
"	7/2/19		Routine and office duties	
"	8/2/19		Inspected animals of 100th Inf Bde Group for demobilization. Routine and office duties	
"	9/2/19		Routine and office duties	
"	10/2/19		Inspected animals of 200th M.G. Batt. for demobilization. Routine and office duties	
"	11/2/19		Inspected the animals of D.H.Q. Routine and office duties	
"	12/2/19		Inspected animals of 100th Inf/Bde, 33 Sigs R.E., Routine & office duties	

WAR DIARY
or
INTELLIGENCE SUMMARY.
(Erase heading not required.)

Army Form C. 2118.

Major R.A.V.C.
D.A.D.V.S.
33 Division

D.A.D.V.S.
33rd DIVISION

Place	Date	Hour	Summary of Events and Information	Remarks and references to Appendices
In the Field	13.2.19		Inspected animals of H.Q.3 and 33 Sig. Coy. R.E.; Routine and office duties	
"	14.2.19		Inspected animals of 200th M.G. Batt.; Routine and office duties	
"	15.2.19		Inspected animals of 19th Inf. Bde.; Routine and office duties	
"	16.2.19		Inspected animals of 100th Inf. Bde.; Routine and office duties	
"	17.2.19		Inspected animals of D.H.Q. and 33 Sig. Coy. R.E. Routine and office duties	
"	18.2.19		Inspected animals at 200th M.G. Batt. Routine and office duties	
"	19.2.19		Visited D.D.V.S., inspected horses of B.H.Q.; Routine and office duties	
"	20.2.19		Routine and office duties	
"	21.2.19		Visited D.D.V.S. Inspected animals of 100th Inf./Bde., Routine + office duties	
"	22.2.19		Visited the Artillery; Routine and office duties	
"	23.2.19		Routine and office duties; Inspected animals of D.H.Q. ends	
"	24.2.19		Routine and office duties. Major G.H. Lowell proceeded on seven days Leave. R.A.V.C. assumed Duties of D.A.D.V.S. During absence of Major Lowell	
"	25.2.19		Routine and office duties	
"	26.2.19		Inspected animals of D.H.Q. and 33rd Sig. Coy. R.E. Visited D.D.V.S.	
"	27.2.19		Routine and office duties	
"	28.2.19		Moved to ETREAT by lorry at 10.00 hours, arriving 16.00 hours	

WAR DIARY or INTELLIGENCE SUMMARY

Army Form C. 2118.

(Erase heading not required.)

of 1st Batt A.S.E Adm. R.V.Y.C
A.D.A.R.V.S
33 Division

OFFICER-IN-CHARGE RECORDS
16 APR 1919
ROYAL ARMY VETY. CORPS.

Place	Date	Hour	Summary of Events and Information	Remarks and references to Appendices
E/PETAT	1.3.19		Located arrivals of 33 Divisional Veterinarian. Routine and office duties	
"	2.3.19		Inspected animals of 33 Div Signal Coy. R.E. Routine and office duties	
"	3.3.19		Routine and office duties	
"	4.2.19		Travelled to arena of work. A.D. Mobile Veterinary Section.	
ANDAINVILLE	5.3.19		Made the necessary arrangements for moving on section to ABBEVILLE in accordance with instructions A.D.V.S 33 Div. N° G.00 dated 3.3.19.	
"	6.3.19		Travelled with my unit. A.3 Mobile Veterinary Section to ABBEVILLE and on arrival handed over the section to O.C. N° 2 Vety Veterinary Hospital, in accordance with D.D.V.S. (Eastern) N° D/M 560 dated 27.2.19 and 33 Div N° G.09 dated 3.3.19.	
E/PETAT	7.3.19		Returned to 33 Divisional Headquarters.	
"	(8) 3.19		Routine and office duties	
"	(9) 12.3.19		Proceeded to N° 5 Veterinary Hospital for duty. (Authority D.D.V.S. (Eastern) N° 35	
"	16.3.19		dated 14.3.19.)	

[signature]
a/Capt R.A.V.C

WAR DIARY
or
INTELLIGENCE SUMMARY.

(Erase heading not required.)

Instructions regarding War Diaries and Intelligence Summaries are contained in F. S. Regs., Part II. and the Staff Manual respectively. Title pages will be prepared in manuscript.

Army Form C. 2118.

OFFICER-IN-CHARGE RECORDS
Major C. J. Farrell. P.A.
16 APR 1919
ROYAL ARMY PAY CORPS.

Place	Date	Hour	Summary of Events and Information	Remarks and references to Appendices
EGRE-TAT	20.3.19		Placed to duty on formation of Divisional Headquarters	
"	21.3.19		Visited all Canteens & Divisional Headquarters doito	
"	10.3.19		Routine and office duties	
"	to 31.3.19			

J. Farrell. Major
R.A.P.C.
33 Division

www.ingramcontent.com/pod-product-compliance
Lightning Source LLC
Chambersburg PA
CBHW081412160426
43193CB00013B/2163